BRITISH PUBLIC FINANCES
THEIR STRUCTURE AND DEVELOPMENT
1880–1952

British Public Finances

THEIR STRUCTURE AND
DEVELOPMENT
1880–1952

URSULA K. HICKS, M.A.

athleen (Webb)

*University Lecturer in
Public Finance, Oxford*

Geoffrey Cumberlege

OXFORD UNIVERSITY PRESS

LONDON   NEW YORK   TORONTO

1954

First published in 1954

Printed in Great Britain by The Riverside Press, Edinburgh

PREFACE

THE structure of a country's finances does not change quickly; the greater part of public revenue is earmarked for continuing expenditure, and in turn must inevitably be raised from existing and well tried taxes. The only exception to this is the occasion of a major war when the expenditure structure has suddenly to be distorted to meet vital yet mainly temporary new demands, while at the same time there is a general willingness to pay extraordinary taxation which would not normally be found. The slowness of major change does not imply that the relatively small adjustments which take place from year to year are not important; they may well be pointers of the utmost significance. But to observe the basic structural changes in public finance it is necessary to take a fairly long period; in no two generations have they been so striking as in the years since 1880.

My chosen period opens just at the termination of the high point of Victorian *laisser-faire* and economy in the public services. The Education Act of 1870 and the important codifying Public Health Act of 1875 were already pointing the way to the modern social services; the establishment of multi-purpose local authorities which were to become Parliament's main agents for carrying them out was just round the corner. On the revenue side the 2d. income tax had only just been left behind, although even Gladstone knew in his heart that the plan for abolishing the tax completely would never be carried out. Indeed the advocates of progressive taxation, at least in the form of a differential against property incomes, were already girding their loins.

My story really ends with 1951, although I have included later statistics where reliable figures were available. The return of the Conservatives to power in the autumn of that year serves to mark the end of a period: the major dislocations to the British economy due to the war had passed over (although this was not immediately apparent); a definite, though restrained, return to the use of credit control in support of fiscal policy was made. At the same time the main outlines of the welfare state had been established and agreed, as well as much of the new apparatus for achieving national balance through a social accounting technique. On the financial side at least the new factors which emerged towards the end of 1951 can in fact be traced in the later months of the Labour government, but the change of control served to emphasize them and so to round off the period.

U. K. H.

Oxford
1954

CONTENTS

TABLES

CHARTS

Chapter I

THE GROWTH OF THE PUBLIC
AUTHORITIES

SEVENTY-TWO years is a long time, although not more than a normal span of life. The generation with which we are concerned has seen many striking changes; above all, perhaps, the use of the internal combustion engine, its application to flying, and its prospective supersession by the jet and gas turbine. In few fields, however, have the changes been more fundamental than in that of public finance, because there we are faced with a complete alteration in the social outlook. In a catchpenny phrase it is a change from the mentality of 'The rich man in his castle, the poor man at his gate, God made them high and lowly and ordered their estate' to a world which accepts equality, not merely of opportunity, but actually of disposable income, as a goal of policy. In another aspect the transition is from the intense individualism of the liberal state to the group consciousness of the welfare state.

This change in outlook has implied a drastic alteration in the balance of the different parts of the economy. That part which undertakes the job of satisfying consumers' individual wants, directly or indirectly, because it expects to make a living in the business—that part, in other words, which statisticians now refer to as 'the private sector'—has shrunk, not absolutely indeed, for the whole process has been accompanied by an enormous rise in the real standard of living, but in relation to the other part, which it is fashionable in the same quarters to refer to as 'the public sector'. Workers in the public sector are indeed also largely engaged in satisfying consumers' wants in some way, but less those wants which are revealed by their own preferences on the market than those which the government chooses for them.

Not merely has the size of the public sector, and hence its demands on the real resources of the economy, expanded enormously, both absolutely and relatively, over the lifetime of our imaginary citizen, but the character of the public services, and even of the authorities which provide them, has changed almost beyond recognition. An exhaustive account of public authorities at different times during our period would take us into detail which would be quite irrelevant to our main task; but a clear idea of the principal components of the public sector and of their relative importance at different stages is necessary for a proper appreciation of the veritable revolution which has come upon us.

The traditional authorities for conducting the business of the public sector which the nineteenth century inherited from an earlier period, were the Home and Foreign departments of the central government (of which the Treasury was already something more than *primus inter pares*), the local justices, the bodies governing certain towns, and the parish vestries. Of these traditional authorities even those which still survive function in ways that are substantially different from their former habits. In default of any general system of elected local authorities, the justices performed a number of administrative duties which would now be carried out by the councils.

Some of the departments of the central government still carried on a substantially independent life; the Navy had been the hardest of all to bring into line, although the Younger Pitt, at the beginning of the nineteenth century, had subjected it to a first round of financial discipline. When our period opens, the process of integrating the work of the Departments with the policy of the government was being completed. On the financial side this was the work mainly of two great Gladstonian institutions (established some twenty years earlier): the Public Accounts Committee in Parliament and its administrative partner, the Department of Exchequer and Audit.

Some, but by no means all, of the borough corporations had undergone a first stage of reform as a result of the Municipal Corporations Act of 1835; even earlier than this several of the new industrial towns had found their more or less village types of government quite inadequate to deal with the urgent social problems posed by their rapid growth, and had promoted private legislation to appoint Improvement Commissioners, exercising many of the functions of modern city councils.

A more notable portent of the shape of things to come had been the creation of Poor Law Unions by the first reformed House of Commons. These were managed by elected Boards of 'Guardians of the Poor', whose very title suggests the existence of a submerged social conscience which was gradually to surface by the end of the nineteenth century. Then there were the local Highway Boards, whose business it was to convert the medieval road system to the needs of more rapid transport, and especially to fit it to feed the great new railway system. In 1870 the School

Boards Act added to the number of ad hoc authorities, and made it possible to fill in the gaps in the existing system of charitable education, thus giving the government its first opportunity of taking a direct hand in educational policy.

Finally, and most prophetic of all, came the Sanitary Boards in 1872, the result of repeated cholera epidemics, and the gradual realization that these were not an Act of God, but the direct consequence of dirt and vermin. The importance of this forward step in public health was that for the first time the entire country was mapped out under the jurisdiction of elected bodies concerned with the welfare of the whole population. Thus the public sector at the beginning of our period consisted of an incoherent motley of authorities, some more or less popularly elected, others resting on a frankly arbitrary although traditional basis. So far as it is possible to speak of public policy at all in respect of home affairs, it was a policy only of individual services, such as education or the relief of the poor.

The decisive step in modernization from the organizational point of view was the creation of the system of popularly elected multi-purpose Local Authorities covering the whole country: County Councils, County Borough Councils, Municipal Borough and District Councils, essentially as we know them today, by legislation extending from 1882 to 1894. This followed rapidly and naturally from the completion of adult male franchise (except for the paupers who got in with the women in 1918). The new local authorities took over the work of the Sanitary Boards, the Highway Boards, and most of the administrative work of the Justices. Once this transfer had been made, we can see with hindsight that it would be only a matter of time before all the ad hoc local bodies were merged in the system of multi-purpose authorities. The School Boards fell in—protesting loudly—in 1902, and finally the Guardians were absorbed in 1929.

The next decisive step in the development of the public sector was the result of the work of the Poor Law Commission, appointed by the Conservatives in 1906 but reporting under the Liberals in 1909. More particularly important for the shape of the public sector was the Minority Report, inspired by the Webbs and the Fabians. The aim of this was the removal of the nineteenth-century stigma of pauperism, and a reversal of the harsh treatment of the poor of the mid-century. The Poor Law was to be 'broken up' by removing from public assistance all groups for whom more appropriate treatment could be found: pensions for the elderly, insurance for the sick and unemployed. Their recommendations in this direction were largely implemented by the ambitious young men of the Liberal government of 1906, Winston Churchill fathering health insurance and Lloyd George unemployment insurance, while old age pensions was the work of their leader, Asquith.

It is especially significant that the pensions and insurance schemes were organized on a national basis; although controlled by ad hoc bodies and not directly under government departments, for the first time a national social policy became possible. This was decisive not merely for the structure, but also for the rate of growth of the public sector. So long as the assistance services were a local responsibility their expansion was limited by the rigidity of local financial resources; a centrally controlled administration could at need draw on the whole national system of finance.

Thus, on the *social* side, the present structure of the public sector was almost complete in outline by the eve of the first world war; it awaited only the absorption of the Guardians (carried out as we have seen in 1929) and the amalgamation of the insurance schemes into an integrated system of social security, finally achieved in 1948.

One more strand in the development of the public sector requires to be noticed, although it only indirectly affected its size: the growth of the central departments responsible for the social services. The early Victorians had created a central department (later known as the Local Government Board) whose primary duty it was to look after poor law administration. As the services of the local authorities widened, the Department's coverage also extended and after the first world war this was recognized in a new name: the Ministry of Health. Since 1945 it has undergone more frequent changes of name, emphasizing now one, now another of its functions, but the Department continues in the old tradition. In 1900 was created the first central department with a definite long-run policy of promoting an integrated national social service: the Board of Education. Thus at the central end, also, the modern structure of the public sector was virtually complete on the side of the social services by 1914. Much rationalization was required, however, before it assumed its present form; the National Insurance Act, for instance, required the repeal of more than thirty measures before an integrated social security system could be established.

Pari passu with the growth of their social duties

the local authorities had gradually been acquiring a series of *economic* powers which were in fact the first steps on the economic side of the development of the public sector. At first boroughs got their powers by ad hoc private Acts, but some national legislation, especially the Electricity Acts, definitely encouraged boroughs to undertake 'municipal trading'. With water, gas, electricity, and trams (not to mention a motley of minor trading services), becoming quite generally attached to their administrative duties, both the character of the local authorities and the size of the public sector were noticeably changed, and in a way that reacted favourably on the standard of local administration, by making the work more interesting.

Last of all, but ultimately most important, came the development of local authority Housing. London and a few of the larger cities had put their hands to the job before 1914, but generalized and compulsory legislation and the regular development of local Housing Departments came only in the 1920s. From the point of view of service, Housing is partly social, partly trading, but from the point of view of the relative importance of the public sector it has had an entirely new significance, through the potentially enormous demands which it creates on the supplies of constructional materials and of specialized labour.

These trading and semi-trading services were different in character from the previous activities of local authorities. For the most part local councils were here engaged on services to be bought voluntarily by consumers in a way that was closely parallel to the services supplied by the private sector. On the whole these services catered for individual and not for collective needs.

For the greater part of our period the Post Office was the only significant economic activity carried on by the central government. Primarily regarded as an administrative service of strategic importance, the Post Office became more definitely a trading service after the purchase of telephone rights from the private sector; but even today the post office services and finances are conducted on a basis that is more administrative than economic in outlook. If we ignore the roads—which might properly have been, but were not, conducted according to an economic plan—no further expansion of the central government's trading activities[1] took place until shortly before the outbreak of the second world war. The Agricultural Marketing Boards as they finally emerged in the later 1930s were the parents of a vast new activity of the public sector: a combined system of commodity dealing and subsidization which reached its maximum in the second world war and the years immediately succeeding it.

On the heels of the second world war came the great spate of nationalization; production and manufacture, as well as trading, now became the responsibility of the public sector on a national basis. Of the four great nationalized industries operating in 1950—coal, transport, electricity, and gas—only the first two were additional to the public sector, and transport not completely at that. Both electricity and gas had been substantially 'socialized' already under municipal ownership for several decades. Thus the process of nationalization implied an important transfer of control within the public sector as well as an

---

[1] Neglecting also the semi-independent Public Corporations, such as the Central Electricity Board, whose position is discussed in the next chapter.

extension of its influence; but the new comers to the public sector—coal and transport—were much the largest of the nationalized industries. For the sake of completeness we should also bear in mind the publicly-owned financial institutions: the traditional savings banks and, from 1946, the Bank of England also. The latter had for long been regarded as a public institution, and for some time previous to nationalization its relations with the Treasury had been so close that *de jure* ownership added little actual power to the public sector. These public credit institutions make negligible demands on the country's supply of real economic resources, but can nevertheless play a vital part in implementing policy.[1]

Thus at the end of our period we should think of the public sector as consisting of (1) the administrative activities of the central departments; (2) the centralized but nominally independent activities of the social security system; (3) the administrative departments of the local authorities, together with the remnant of their trading services left by the tide of nationalization, above all their housing departments; and (4) the economic activities of certain central departments (such as the Board of Trade and Ministry of Food) and of the great nationalized industries.

The picture that emerges is much more coherent and unified than anything which had previously been seen; but, significantly, it is one in which the central government not only makes direct demands on a very substantial—even predominant—share of the economy's supply of economic resources, but also, by its control on the one side of the supply and distribution of fuel, power and transport, and on the other of the country's

[1] See Chapter VI.

financial institutions, plays, for good or ill, a pre-dominant part in the direction of economic life.

A quantitative picture of the change in structure which underlies this revolution in the size and significance of the public sector, and which is directly relevant to our subject, can be obtained by watching the course of change over our period in the size of the public sector in relation to the total of all incomes in the economy (the net national income). Although this proportion does not precisely indicate the *real* changes that have taken place, since it inevitably measures flows of money and not of the real goods and services which money could buy, it does provide a reasonably good idea of the strength of the demands of the public sector at different periods on the economic resources of the economy, since it automatically makes allowance for changes in the value of money and for the growth of population.

Chart I shows the proportion which total current public expenditure bore to national income over the whole of our period. Public expenditure covers the current expenditure of the central government (including the insurance funds) and of local authorities, as well as the gross expenditure on current account of public trading services. This is not, of course, a complete record of the demands of the public sector on economic resources; we need to include also expenditure on fixed assets [1] and stocks of raw materials and finished products; but for the moment we may concentrate on the current account.

In interpreting Chart I it must be borne in mind that short-period changes in the relation between

[1] See below, pp. 19 ff.

CHART I

PUBLIC EXPENDITURE AS A
PERCENTAGE OF THE NATIONAL INCOME
(Including gross current expenditure of Local Trading
Services but excluding Public Corporations)

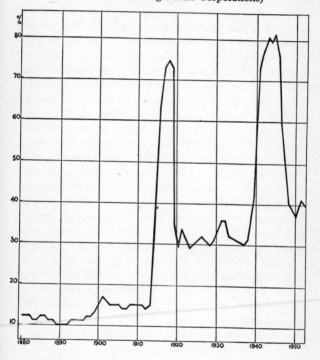

public expenditure and the national income may have no particular relevance for the long-period growth of the public sector, although they may be of the utmost importance for budgetary policy and for questions of economic stabilization. Public expenditure reacts in different ways to changes in the national income; but on the whole, and especially in the past, there has been a tendency for expenditure to expand in good times, although to a less degree than the rise in the national income (so that the proportion tended to fall), and to contract in times of depression, but not by so much as the fall in the national income, owing to the rigid nature of contractual expenditure (so that the proportion tended to rise). In Chart I the boom years—for instance 1906, 1913, 1928, and 1936—clearly conform to this rule, as do, in the opposite direction, the depression years of the early '30s.

Even allowing for this factor, and neglecting the periods of the two major wars, two things emerge clearly from the steady upsurge of the public sector revealed by the chart. In the first place the period divides very definitely into three sub-periods: (1) up to 1913, when the outlay of the public sector did not exceed 15 per cent. of the national income; (2) the inter-war years when the norm had risen to a little over 30 per cent.; (3) the years since the end of the second world war, when it seems pretty clear that a norm of about 40 per cent.[1] has been established. On closer inspection we might plausibly divide the first sub-period into two stages: (i) the 1880s and 1890s,

[1] The transfer of local trading services to public corporations implies that on a strictly comparable basis the figures for the most recent years should be slightly higher; in any case they can only be regarded as provisional.

when a percentage of 10 or 11 was normal; and (*ii*) the first decade of the present century when 14 per cent. or 15 per cent. was the rule. Although this difference seems small by later standards, it was, as we shall see, of very real significance.

Secondly we see that the change in level in every case followed on war. The 1870s were a period of relative calm; income tax touched its lowest level of 2d. in the pound; defence expenditure was as low as £26 mn. But the 1880s were troubled by a number of wars and rumours of wars: in the Transvaal and Bechuanaland, in the Sudan and on the Afghan frontier. In 1886 defence was costing half as much again as it had cost in 1870; but, although a slight upward stirring is discernible, the position of the public sector seems to have been remarkably stable for about three decades prior to the outbreak of the Boer War. The change which followed this—still minor—operation is far more definite. It is clear that a new level of public expenditure was already established before the whole picture was distorted by the outbreak of the first world war.

It would be going too far to claim that the marked changes in the size of the public sector which followed on war resulted from it,[1] because there were clearly many other causes at work also; but in an important sense wars have been responsible. On the one side the high level of taxation which can be established in wartime, almost without protest, conditions taxpayers to permanently higher exactions; on the other side in

[1] Apart from the interest on the expanded national debt, which is different in kind from 'real' expenditure, and is perhaps better regarded as negative public income rather than as positive public outlay.

wartime the activities of the public sector (or rather of the central government) expand enormously, and at the end of the war the receding tide, no matter how fast it flows, inevitably leaves some new responsibilities behind it. This was especially true of the second world war, when in addition to new activities directly reflected in a rise in public outlay, a large part of the structure of wartime control, and rationing was continued long after the close of hostilities and used for the purpose of implementing the government's social and economic policy.

Yet although the recurrent need for defence expenditure has been the occasion of repeated expansions of the public sector, there is no very conclusive evidence that it is itself a cause of permanent expansion; its claim to be such a cause is set out in Table I, tracing in selected years over our period the importance of defence, both in relation to total central expenditure

TABLE I

Expenditure on Defence
(Selected Years)

Year	As Percentage of Total Central Current Expenditure	As Percentage of Net National Income
1880	33	2·5
1890	38	2·4
1895	39	2·6
1905	41	3·3
1913	38	3·7
1923	14	2·7
1933	14	2·8
1938	22	5·3
1948	22	7·5
1950	25	6·9

and to national income. Although it is true that in 1890 only 2·4 per cent. of the national income was used up in this way, while in 1950 6·9 per cent. was required, in the inter-war years of the twentieth century the percentage devoted to defence was hardly larger than at the close of the nineteenth century; again the relative rate of reduction after the second world war was no less rapid than after the first. Much more striking is the decline in the importance of defence expenditure in the budget; it swallowed up 38 per cent. of central government outlay in 1890, 41 per cent. in 1905, but only 22 per cent. in 1948. Although this fall has a significance of its own, it is of course mainly the reflexion of the expansion of other forms of outlay.

The major explanation of the growth of the public sector has been, as is indeed well realized, the expansion of the social services. From 1·6 per cent. of the national income (or 14·4 per cent. of total public outlay) in 1890 social expenditure had risen to about 14 per cent. of the national income (or over 38 per cent. of total public outlay) by 1950. We might very well also include expenditure on general food subsidies (4 per cent. of the national income in 1950) since after the end of the war the 'social' element in these steadily expanded. The rise in 'constructive' social services (as we might call them, in contrast to the 'rescue' services of unemployment pay and public assistance) has been even greater than these figures suggest. In the inter-war period a large proportion of social expenditure (over 30 per cent. in 1935) was taken up by the rescue services; in 1950 they required little more than 4 per cent. In the next chapter we shall have to investigate the genesis of these most significant changes; here we need only note that as the national income per head has risen the nation has chosen to devote an increasingly large proportion of its resources to social betterment. In all this there has certainly been no logical development, either of the services as a whole or in their relative importance. We may however say that development has taken place through a fully democratic process of ascertaining the strength of demand through a process of legislative trial and error.

Hardly less striking is the change which has occurred over our period in the attitude to the economic activities of public authorities, and in the scope of those activities themselves. From the last decade of the nineteenth century the traditional local trading services began to develop, and were soon rapidly expanding. Their importance rose from 2·3 per cent. of the national income in 1913 to 4·5 per cent. in 1938. In the years since 1945 this growth has been abruptly checked by the transfer of local electricity, gas, and tramway undertakings to national ownership. The establishment of the nationalized industries, together with the expansion of the trading activities of government departments and agencies (such as the Raw Cotton Commission), brought the total of gross current public expenditure on production and trading to 18·4 per cent. of the national income in 1948. (In the most recent years, however, some of these trading activities have been dismantled.) On investment account the expansion has been even more striking, as we shall presently see. In addition to production and trading by public authorities, state aid to different sections of agriculture and industry, non-existent before the inter-war period, had risen from £14 mn. in 1938 to £94 mn. in 1948. (In this sphere also there has since been some small decline.) Moreover, the expenditure has been much more influential than the figures suggest, since it has been backed up by a large array of controls and allocations.

Traditionally the social services, and indeed the economic activities of the public sector (other than the Post Office) were mainly the business of the local authorities. It was held that local organization would be more closely in touch with individual needs and demands. From the time of the establishment of the social insurance funds at the end of the first decade of the twentieth century the process of local expansion has tended to be reversed. All the newer social services have been set up on a national basis, with the exception of Housing, and in respect of this there is very strong central control. As a result of this process, and more recently of the loss of their major trading services, local authorities have gradually lost ground, not only in relation to the central government, but recently in respect of their position in the national economy. In 1880, before the great development of social services and trading activities, local expenditure amounted to over 42 per cent. of total public outlay; by 1950 it had declined to about 15 per cent. The great period of local activity was the first decade of the present century: of recent years local expenditure has declined in relation to the national income; between 1938 and 1948 it fell from just over 9 per cent. to just over 7 per cent.

Thus, in spite of the relative decline in defence expenditure (which is peculiarly the business of the central government), a strong tendency to centralization is apparent, *pari passu* with the growth of the public sector. This is partly the result of war: the central government tends to increase its powers during emergencies, not only *vis-à-vis* the private sector, but in relation also to local authorities, whose work, in contrast, tends at such times to contract. The increasing degree of centralization is also partly deliberate, the reflection of a greater emphasis on uniformity of standards and of a stronger desire for a national policy in the socio-economic field.

The changes in the structure of public expenditure have been accompanied by a change in its character. The primary purpose of government expenditure, the satisfaction of wants that are not only collective by nature, but can only be collectively supplied (such as police and justice as well as defence), has declined relatively to the satisfaction of individual wants. Even within the framework of social expenditure, which is primarily concerned with individual satisfactions, there has been a similar shift of emphasis.

Apart from public assistance, expenditure on which is primarily governed by the level of economic activity, the first social services to attain any importance were education and public health provisions of the nature of sewerage and cleansing services, services which are almost as much of communal as of individual benefit. More recently the expansion of the social services has all been in the direction of services accruing directly to particular citizens (for instance pensions and the national health service), and ardently desired by them, as a means of individual satisfaction—more especially perhaps when the benefits come in the form of direct money payments.

A similar shift of emphasis seems to be discernible also on the side of economic expenditure. The newer trading services—domestic gas and electricity supplies, and more especially the services of the nationalized industries in contrast to water supply or street lighting —tend to be concerned with sales to individuals and firms exactly parallel to services supplied by the private sector. The increased scope of expenditure in aid of particular industries is a further instance of the growth of individual, or more precisely group, benefits accruing from public outlay.

This shift in the character of public expenditure is of very great significance for the general attitude to the public sector. More and more there are individual or group benefits to be obtained, benefits in which certain citizens (for instance pensioners) or industries have a vested interest, and whose expansion will improve their personal or profit prospects. In this situation the largesse of the welfare state becomes something to be striven for, in the same way as an increase in wages or a tax concession on a certain type of profits.

The public expenditure which we have so far been considering consists of outlay on goods and services for current use or consumption; but expenditure on capital account is also of great and growing importance. In a sense its expansion is even more significant than the expansion of current expenditure, for it represents the assumption of responsibilities which are largely new to the public sector. In the nineteenth century, apart from the occasional purchase of existing assets (such as the shares of the Suez Canal Co.) the investment activities of the central government were confined to the development of the postal system, including telegraphs and telephones. Expenditure on highway development which might well have been considered a capital item never has been so regarded, to the detriment of the efficiency of our road system. From the closing years of the nineteenth century, however, local trading services began to call for considerable amounts of fixed capital formation; there was also a growing investment in non-trading assets such as schools, sewerage works, and municipal buildings. In the inter-war period these investment activities were entirely eclipsed by the expansion of local authority housing.

The end of the second world war was quickly followed by the establishment of the basic nationalized industries; in the first instance existing assets were

TABLE 2

Public and Private Gross Fixed Capital Formation at Home
(£mn.)   (Calendar Years)

Year	1913	1938	1948 [1]	1949 [1]	1950 [1]	1951 [1]
Central Government (including Nationalized Industries) .	4	34	286	377	416	515
Local Authorities .	23	206	384	384	411	444
Total Public . .	27	240	670	761	827	959
Private (Personal and Company) . .	?	530	723	773	847	904
Total Capital Formation						
at Current Prices .	..	770	1393	1534	1674	1863
at 1948 Prices .	..	1155	1393	1491	1562	1545
Public Capital Formation						
as a Percentage of the Total . .	..	31	48	49	49	51

[1] From *National Income and Expenditure*, 1946–52.

acquired from the private sector or from the trading departments of local authorities, but in all cases it was realized that a large volume of new investment would have to follow. Table 2 shows the relative importance not only of central and local investment in the public sector, but also of the public and private sectors respectively. It will be seen that the growth of local relative to central investment in the inter-war period was no less striking than the growth of central relative to local after the establishment of the nationalized industries.

Official figures are not available before 1938, but it is evident that public has rapidly been overhauling private investment and in this too the decision to nationalize has been vital. At the same time, when the figures are revalued at constant prices the increase is not spectacular; between 1948 and 1951 there was a rise of only 10 per cent. To some extent special causes of physical shortage have held down the volume of investment in both the public and the private sectors since 1945, but the slow rate of expansion, especially in the public industries with their heavy problems of rationalization and integration, is nevertheless disturbing.

It goes without saying that the expansion of the public sector which we have so far regarded from the outlay side is reflected on the tax side also; indeed the three stages of expansion are even more precisely marked here than on the outlay side. Revenue collections on the whole pursue a steadier course, less interrupted by short period fluctuations than expenditure. Up to the first world war tax revenue averaged about 10 per cent. of the national income; in the

inter-war period the norm had risen to about
25 per cent. and since 1945 a norm of something like
40 per cent. is apparent.

The increase in total revenue has been accompanied
by a marked change in its composition. Income and
capital taxes (death duties), which were relatively
insignificant in Gladstone's day (15 per cent. of total
tax revenue in 1885), had expanded to 47 per cent.
by 1950; during the war they had been very much
higher. The change in the character of these taxes
through the introduction of progression (beginning
with death duties in the early 'nineties), and through
the extension (early in the second world war) of income
tax to include a large proportion of weekly wage
earners, is of even greater significance; but we must
postpone discussion of these factors until Chapter III.
It is worth noting here however that the tendency of
the fiscal system which we saw on the outlay side
to discriminate between different groups and industries
has made its way into the tax system also. A most
important step in this direction was taken by the
reintroduction of protective import duties in 1932;
more recently the same influence has been manifest in
purchase tax. Increasing differences between particular
groups and industries in respect of rebates and reliefs
in income tax have also been made.

It is noticeable further that an even stronger tendency
to centralization is evident on the tax than on the
expenditure side. The local rate, which has a special
significance as the only substantial independent source
of revenue available to local authorities, declined
from a norm of over 30 per cent. of total tax revenue
before 1913 to one of about 17 per cent. in the inter-war
period, and from 1946 to 1950 did not exceed 7 per cent.

In relation to the national income rate revenue fell from over 4 per cent. to under 3 per cent. between 1938 and 1948. At this level it differs very little from its position in the 1880s before the modern development of local government. The difference in the position of the local authorities on the outlay and on the tax sides *vis-à-vis* the central government is of course accounted for by the extensive system of exchequer grants which has grown up over our period; these are matters which we shall have to investigate in Chapter IV.

The change—amounting almost to a revolution—whose outward structure we have been examining factually is not unique to Britain; some, perhaps most, of its features are to be found in virtually every country, more particularly in the countries of Western Europe. Even those, such as the U.S.A., which cling most faithfully to the nineteenth-century tradition of individualism have experienced a notable growth in the functions of the state. Since the end of the second world war the public sector in the United States (measured in terms of the relation of taxation to national income) seemed—at least before the Korean emergency impinged on the economy—to have settled down to something like the 25-30 per cent. level in relation to the national income, which characterized Britain in the inter-war period. This change has been marked by a considerable expansion of the social services, although against continued opposition in some quarters; it has also been accompanied by a conspicuous growth of the activities of the federal government relatively to that of the states.

The revolution in Britain is nevertheless particularly interesting, because although the swing over our period has been greater than in most countries, it has been carried through with remarkable unanimity, almost on what the Americans would call a 'bipartisan' basis. It will facilitate later judgement if we focus attention for a moment on some of the more striking aspects of the change for, as one recent writer has put it, 'the revolution in public finance has been the means of a revolution in society'.[1]

Of most significance of all perhaps is the change in the attitude of the generality of citizens to the activities of the public sector, and hence to public expenditure. To Gladstonian England government was the means whereby society satisfied its basic collective needs, for justice and defence, at home and abroad. Taxes represented an unavoidable but regrettable transfer of resources for this purpose from more fruitful uses, including in the forefront the raising of the general standard of living by personal effort. The social services were at first tolerated because the need for them was assumed only to be temporary. In these circumstances it was obviously desirable to spend on the activities of the government as little as was compatible with their adequate performance. Hence the forces of liberality and progress were thrown heavily on the side of economy in the public services.

We owe a great debt to Gladstone for establishing a well-founded system for the control of public expenditure; for, with the expansion of the public sector, the urgency of avoiding waste has become greater than ever. But it cannot reasonably be denied that the rapid development of the social services, and of the progressive principle in taxation, when it came, was partly the reaction from the Grand Old Man's obstinate

[1] Bertrand de Jouvenal: *The Ethics of Redistribution.*

clinging for so long to economy at any price, even at the price of the primary needs of defence. In the anxious years of the middle 1880s it became clear that this policy would no longer serve; public expenditure must needs expand to meet the calls of defence. At the time it seemed only that the country had been driven off the 'tuppenny income tax', and that Gladstone was finally thrown out of his plan for abolishing the tax completely. With hindsight we can perceive the significance of the discovery that income tax on a permanent basis was after all compatible with national prosperity and expansion.

As we have seen, the new urge for expansion of the public services after the retirement of Gladstone is apparent even on the small scale of Chart I. From 1888 the activities of the new local authorities were steadily growing; 1894 saw the acceptance of the progressive principle in direct taxation. Although for the moment it was confined to death duties, a concrete proposal for its extension to income tax had already been prepared within the heart of Gladstone's own party. The dictum of its author, Harcourt, that 'we are all socialists now' did no more than record the new outlook, in a world where public expenditure was becoming respectable and even desirable. The state had set its foot upon the road which has led to its becoming primarily an agent of social and economic development.

Yet in the longer sweep of history it can plausibly be argued that it was the Gladstone era which was out of the normal line of development. With greatly enhanced wealth and opportunity, it is true, the new policy, it may be said, did no more than pick up again the threads of the sort of state the eighteenth century and early nineteenth century had envisaged. Even Adam Smith, for all his individualism, had stressed the importance of the 'third duty' for the state—beyond justice and arms—of developing public works for 'facilitating the commerce of society and promoting instruction of the people'. Public assistance at the beginning of the nineteenth century, under the Speenhamland 'system', had been a crude but genuine effort to maintain a minimum standard of living, in conditions of inflation such as the Victorians never had to struggle with. The primary development of transport and communications remains today in underdeveloped countries (as England was in 1790) a service for which the state must needs take ultimate responsibility.

Thus the economic duties of the state, which today seems a notable innovation, were in reality very early recognized. Even in late Victorian times the tide of municipal socialization of the public utilities was flowing hardly less strongly than the tide of social reform. The two aspects of the economic activities of the state which are substantially new are, first, the acceptance (in practice if not so openly in principle) of the contention that the state has a right and duty to discriminate in favour of particular branches of industry—as we have seen this cannot be dated much before the 1930s; secondly, the assumption of responsibility for maintaining economic stability at a high level of economic activity. Given the economic analysis which makes this policy in any way practicable (which is itself very modern) this function follows with easy logic from the earlier economic responsibilities of the state. It is notable that it is as readily accepted in the still individualistic United States as in Britain.

It is, however, on the tax side that the change from 1880 has been most momentous. Welfare costs money, and to an important degree the cost must inevitably come from the pockets of the same income groups as the beneficiaries—by lateral transfers from the working to the retired population, from the strong to the weakly, and from the childless to the family. Nevertheless it is inevitably on those with higher than average income or wealth that the responsibility for financing the enlarged public sector mainly falls.

The change from a maximum rate of income tax of 2d. in the pound in the 1870s to an effective maximum of over 19s. 7d. in the pound in 1950 is too great for the imagination easily to grasp its implications; but it is implied that since 1941 there has been a definite ceiling of between £7000 and £8000 above which spendable income cannot rise. To look at the matter another way, the impact of a 2s. 6d. initial rate of tax, followed by successive increments up to 9s. 6d.—not to mention surtax—may only too easily cause the taxpayer to reconsider the respective attractions of work and leisure to the detriment of work, in a way in which a tax of some fraction of a shilling would be most unlikely to do. The bogey of Victorian Chancellors was that if exploited too far in normal times income tax revenue would fail to expand adequately in an emergency. Because they cried 'wolf' so much too soon it would be rash to overlook the reality of the danger inherent in present tax rates. Income tax has come perilously near its limits on the upper incomes, while the extension of the tax to include large numbers of weekly wage earners implies inflationary dangers of compensatory wage demands which are an entirely new factor.

Up to the present probably the most important consequence of the changed position of direct taxation (including the effect of profits tax and progressive death duties with an effective level of 80 per cent. on the largest estates) is not so much the levelling of disposable incomes, which after all is just one aspect of the passion for equality which has swept the country from the beginning of the second world war, but rather the effect on saving. Personal saving has virtually disappeared; Victorian England relied on personal saving for the provision of industrial capital, especially risk capital. The failure of this source implies not merely a reduction in the volume of spontaneous saving out of a given national income, but also a change in the type of saving that can be made available, both of which can hardly fail to be detrimental to the trying out of new projects. The international aspects of this change are hardly less serious than the internal.

A great part of the responsibility for filling the gap in the supply of savings now inevitably falls on the government, either directly through budgetary policy or indirectly through tax concessions to firms who will undertake it. It is precisely to deal with the problem of insufficient savings that the new technique of using the national income as an instrument of policy has been developed; this is a matter which we shall have to examine in Chapter V. The changes in the financial structure which this aspect of the revolution in public finance have brought about are hardly less important than the changes in the social structure.

The welfare state as we now understand it has been in existence in Britain for only a few years. So far as it has gone, and in spite of certain obvious inconveniences, it is clearly generally acceptable. Up to the present indeed its benefits have been more conspicuous than its inconveniences; it is not generally realized how much of this is due to substantial help from abroad. It will be our task in the following pages to analyze the various aspects of the revolution in more detail, as a basis for an evaluation of the type of fiscal adjustments which will be required in the longer period.

Chapter II

THE FORMS OF PUBLIC
EXPENDITURE

IN the last chapter we saw that, apart from the greater needs of defence in our unquiet age, the expansion of the public sector was due to two causes: the growth of social expenditure and the re-establishment of economic activities and policy as an accepted function of the state. Expenditure on defence is a technical matter which it is difficult for the layman to criticize. The most the economist can hope to do is to enquire into the means available for checking that, given certain decisions, the money has been wisely laid out, and to a considerable extent even this can only be discovered by the test of war. Of recent years the Select Committee on the Estimates has devoted special attention to examining defence expenditure, although handicapped by an obsolete system of Accounts. We shall have something to say on their activities at a later stage; our business in the present chapter is to examine the genesis and content of the expansion of social and economic expenditure.

We have seen[1] that expenditure on the social services as a whole grew from less than 2 per cent. of the national income in 1890 to about 18 per cent. (including the general food subsidies) in 1950. Table 3 traces broadly the relative fortunes of the major social services over the period. To start with, over 90 per cent. of public outlay on the social services was devoted to two

[1] See p. 151 above.

TABLE 3

The Relative Importance of the Major Social Services
Current Expenditure in Selected Years (£mn.)
(Figures in Brackets denote Percentages of the National Income)

Year	Education	Public Health and National Health Service	Housing	Assistance and Extended Benefit	Non Contributory Pensions (Civil and War)	Social Security	Nutrition and School Meals	New Services	Total
1890	11·5 (0·8)	1·4 (0·1)	0·2	9·1	..	..	..	..	22·2
1900	19·3 (1·1)	2·8 (0·1)	0·5	12·3	..	..	..	..	34·9
1910	33·5 (1·5)	4·7 (0·2)	1·5	16·1	7·4	..	..	..	63·2
1923	87·4 (2·2)	44·4 (1·1)	16·5	34·3	92·3	41·2 (1·0)	..	..	316·1
1933	101·7 (2·7)	58·6 (1·5)	44·8	85·1	64·9	67·9 (1·8)	..	..	423·1
1936	115·1 (2·5)	65·3 (1·4)	43·8	94·0	87·0	129·0 (2·9)	..	3·9	538·1
1949	267·5 (2·5)	403·7 (3·8)	67·2	68·0 [1]	108·8 (3·8)	398·2 (3·8)	63·0	77·8 [2]	1454·2
1951	344·5 (3·0)	448·8 (4·0)	74·1	92·8 [1]	101·3	428·0 (3·8)	65·0	87·3 [2]	1641·8

[1] Of which National Assistance = 1949, 63; 1951, 88·7.
[2] Of which Family Allowances = 1949, 62·6; 1951, 65·0; Child Care = 1949, 13·5; 1951, 18·9.

purposes: Education (in Victorian language 'Public Instruction') and Relief of the Poor. A small amount was also spent on health services, mainly on the provision of mental hospitals. Then, and until much later, private charity was the sole provider of general hospitals; only the mental patient and the pauper were a charge on public funds.

At the end of our period education still held its place as a major social service (accounting for 20 per cent. of the expenditure in 1951), but relief of the poor (now known as national assistance) had shrunk to a quite minor place (5 per cent. of the total in 1951). This was of course mainly the result of the development of social security with its statutory unemployment pay and other contractual payments; partly, however, it reflects the full employment situation of the years since 1940. In the meantime other services had arisen: housing and expanded health services in the inter-war period, family allowances, additional care of children and above all the national health service in the years since 1945. The war legacy of general food subsidies was closely analogous to this expenditure but was not counted formally among the social services, since it was uncertain how much of the apparatus would be put on to a permanent footing.

Few if any of these services shows any sign of having reached a limit of demand; on the contrary they are typically what the Americans call 'open-ended': at the subsidized price at which the services are offered there is no apparent limit to demand. Hence total expenditure on a service, and its relation to other services, cannot depend on technical considerations (except in so far as these can be artificially introduced, for instance by defining the permissible

number of pupils per teacher or persons per room).
Hence policy decisions are operative in every case.
Thus a very heavy responsibility rests on Parliament,
often in the face of strong vested interests, to secure
an appropriate development of the different services
on the one hand and a reasonable balance between
social expenditure and other public needs on the other.

Within the space available it is obviously impossible
to attempt a detailed survey of the social services;
nevertheless a brief examination of the development
of the major services and of the policy underlying
it seems essential for an understanding of present
policy trends. We shall therefore sketch in turn the
fortunes of the major services (those costing more
than £300 mn., either on current or capital account,
in 1950), namely: Education, Social Security, including
Health and Pensions, Housing, and the Food Subsidies.

Of all the social services Education is the one in
which a consistent long-term policy has longest and
most steadily been followed by those responsible for
the administration. It is as well that this has been so
since education was never an aggressive social service;
it is not one for which the beneficiaries—or their
parents—are as a rule prepared to fight hard. For this
reason perhaps education has usually been the first
victim of economy campaigns, and these in turn have
hampered its orderly development. Thus it is not
surprising that in relation to the national income
public expenditure on schooling has only risen
moderately over the years since the early '20s (3 per
cent. in 1951 as compared with 2·2 per cent. in 1923);
in relation to the other social services it has lost
ground steadily.

Public policy in education effectively dates from the Act of 1870, because although grants had been made much earlier in aid of charitable effort, now for the first time a special rate could be imposed for educational purposes, and, further, this could be supplemented by a system of grants from the exchequer, making a national policy practicable. Almost from the first the education grants developed a double-headed aim: to raise the standard of performance by the carrot-and-stick method, but at the same time to make allowance for local difficulties, especially those of poor areas. The establishment of a central department in 1900 and the abolition of the ad hoc school boards in 1902 (so that education became the business of the ordinary local authorities) greatly facilitated the development of a national policy.

The history of the development of education policy divides naturally into three phases: (1) from the (Forster) Act of 1870 to 1914; (2) from the (Fisher) Act of 1918 to the eve of the second world war, and (3) the latest phase dating from the (Butler) Act of 1944; thus education expenditure conforms closely to the timing of the expansion of the social services in general.

The early administrators inevitably concentrated their attention on the 'Three R's', more specifically on attaining 100 per cent. literacy; nevertheless from a very early period the need for full development of the child's capacities, both physical and intellectual, has explicitly been present in statements of official policy. On the physical side from 1907 it became possible for local education authorities to provide meals for undernourished children—it having been discovered that many children were physically unable to take advantage of the opportunities offered to them.

In 1908 the Children's Act gave special protection against neglect, exploitation, and ill treatment. Even more important than these was the development of the school medical services, legislation for which dates from 1907, but from 1913 inspection and treatment were greatly stimulated by the provision of a specific grant. From these small beginnings have developed the present important nutrition and child care services, as well as the special schools for handicapped children. If these services be added to the direct expenditure on normal education, as would be not unreasonable, education in a broad sense had considerably more than maintained its place in the national economy.

On the intellectual side the achievement of the administrators between 1890 and 1910 was the establishment of a universal and compulsory system of primary education—the last fees in elementary schools were abolished by the Fisher Act. Education above the elementary level, however, figured in policy from an early date. It was first sought in technical schools (under legislation of 1889) whose vocational curricula were selected ad hoc rather than in relation to the main stream of public education. From 1907, however, free places were made available in secondary schools for exceptional pupils from the elementary schools. The idea of a national system of universal secondary education, although present from an early date in the century, did not find its way on to the statute book until the Fisher Act; even now it has not been fully achieved.

In the first stage of policy universal literacy had been attained; the achievement of the inter-war period was undoubtedly the generalization, if not the universalization, of secondary education. This constituted a major step forward in educational policy. State-aided or state-provided secondary schools became for the first time the leading factor in post-primary education in the country. The importance of the change that had taken place was immediately apparent in the second world war: a trained and disciplined public was available, not only to operate the complicated machinery of modern defence, but also for the scarcely less complicated requirements of civilian life under total war conditions. The second world war was won not so much on the playing fields of Eton (although the status of the Public Schools had not actually declined) as in the classrooms of the public elementary and secondary schools.

The importance of the new secondary education was seen no less in the type of student entering the universities; for the first time in the 1930s the talent of the country was being effectively mobilized by drawing on the state secondary schools and aided grammar schools as well as on the traditional public schools. Important as this achievement was it can reasonably be criticized in that the system of education provided was still only really appropriate for the limited number of intellectually outstanding adolescents for whom it had initially been planned; it would not well bear generalization over the whole school population. In particular the war revealed the much greater effectiveness of technical training elsewhere, especially in the U.S.A.

The Butler Act of 1944 opened a new phase in educational policy, although its application was inevitably delayed by the final stages of the war. This aims at universal secondary education, emphasized by the compulsory raising of the school leaving age to 15 (already abortively attempted both by the Fisher Act and by the (Trevelyan) Act of 1930) and by the abolition of fees in secondary schools. On the basis of the development which had already taken place in the 1930s this implies concentration on secondary education for the normally and subnormally gifted child, in contrast to the above-average child who was already fairly well catered for.

While admirable as a policy, and indeed no more than the logical development of what had gone before, the full implementation of the Butler system is fraught with considerable difficulties, by no means all of a strictly financial nature. It will inevitably be very expensive both in terms of schools [1] and of teachers, if only because the normal and subnormal are so much more numerous than the gifted. If funds cannot easily be found for all there is a real danger of the neglect of the gifted child, who after all presents the most fruitful field for education, and from whose ranks the leaders of the future must come. The experience of other countries suggests that in education it is fatally easy to sacrifice quality for quantity. In Britain this danger is emphasized by the financial difficulties of the traditional Public Schools—the best of which have always concentrated on fitting the training exactly to the capacities of the child—due to the heavy taxation of middle class parents.

Secondly, the Butler policy implies a substantial increase in the centralization of educational administration, and hence to a considerable extent of policy. The educational powers of the county Districts have

---

[1] A forthright Report of the Estimates Committee in June 1953 emphasized that this problem had not yet been adequately faced.

been taken away, and administration concentrated under the less numerous (and hence more easily controlled) authorities of county council status. Further, in the interests of a uniform policy, the Minister has been given much wider powers than ever before, powers of direction and of the withholding of grants for various reasons, including deviations from national policy. The significance of these powers is enhanced by a very great increase in the exchequer grants for education.

In no part of the educational system is this change more apparent than in the relations between the state and the universities. It is now exceptional for a student to come up to the university without state aid (73 per cent. were so assisted in 1950); not only have the grants made by the exchequer to the governing bodies of universities increased more than eightfold,[1] but in effect they now extend to the constituent Colleges of the older universities as well as to the Faculties. This is a situation in which, no doubt, university training for the many becomes much more practicable, but it carries with it dangers of a control which might spell loss of initiative and freedom which could be fatal for the advancement of knowledge. Happily up to the present these dangers remain a mere potentiality.

The relief of poverty is by far the oldest of the public social services, dating from the time of Elizabeth I and even earlier. The direction of policy has however been very different from that of education. As education has always been the most centralized of the social services administered locally, so public

[1] 65 per cent. of University income now comes from the state as compared with 34 per cent. in the middle 1930s.

assistance has been the most decentralized. There have indeed been three important declarations of policy by the central government, the results of which in turn set the stage during the years succeeding them; but the development has been played out with much local variety and often very far from the intentions of Whitehall.

At the beginning of our period the code of the 'New' Poor Law, as established by legislation in 1833, inspired by Chadwick and Senior, was still in operation. Its emphasis was heavily on the treatment of the pauper as less than a normal citizen, and on the avoidance of relief in the home as far as possible. From 1909, as we have seen, largely due to the work of the Fabians, an entirely new approach captured the field, aiming at a practical reversal of Chadwick's ideas. The third declaration of policy, that embodied in the (Beveridge) Report of the Interdepartmental Committee on Social Insurance and Allied Services of 1942, although revolutionary in many respects, must properly be regarded as a logical development of the ideas which had already been made explicit in 1909.

Although the austerity of the 'new' poor law code was from an early date (and well before the opening of our period) considerably softened in practice by the natural humanity of the Guardians who administered it, policy continued to be dominated by two (not very openly acknowledged) aims: to protect the rest of the community from a potentially criminal class of able-bodied paupers, and to secure the relief of destitution at minimum cost.

Thus, in a period when other social services were increasingly being aided by grants from the exchequer, Treasury assistance towards the relief of the poor was steadily refused. This had the result of minimizing the costs to the community in general, since local resources of the areas most affected were strictly limited; but it also resulted in the development of very varying standards of relief between rich and poor areas, and at the same time led to an intolerable burden of poor rates in the poorer areas. These difficulties were intensified when after 1918 the political disabilities on paupers were removed and the 'pauper vote' became of importance in local politics.

As we have seen, the 1909 Report aimed at the removal of the stigma of pauperism and at the 'break up of the poor law' by removing from public charity all those who could appropriately be aided on more self-respecting lines. A small beginning had been made in this direction by the Workmen's Compensation Act of 1897, the scope of which was much extended in 1906. This gave assistance for industrial injuries entirely outside the range of poor relief. The main implementation of the new policy however came (as we have seen) with the three notable liberal reforms of the early years of the twentieth century: Old Age Pensions (at 70 with a Means Test), in 1908, in 1912 National Health Insurance and a limited scheme of Unemployment Insurance. The heavy unemployment which succeeded the first world war led directly to the extension of unemployment insurance in 1920, and indirectly to the introduction of contributory pensions in 1925 (at 65 and 60 for the insured worker and his wife or widow respectively). Both these extensions were carried by Conservative governments; but in 1925 Winston Churchill who had played such a leading part in the establishment of social insurance in the second decade of the century, was the Conservative Chancellor of the Exchequer.

Thus the foundations of the present social security system were already laid early in the inter-war period. When the Interdepartmental Committee came to examine the situation in 1942 it found a social security system in operation superior to that of most countries (save perhaps in respect of direct cash payments); nevertheless a number of difficult problems had emerged in the thirty years of operation.

Unemployment insurance in particular had been in repeated difficulties through the 1920s; if contributions were moderate the fund was in chronic danger of insolvency; if they were raised they constituted a severe tax on employers and the employed. If assistance was moderate, in order to relieve the fund, the unemployed, especially the long unemployed, would be thrown back again on public assistance with all its local vagaries, just what it was desired to avoid. On the other hand if assistance was more generous, for the man with a large family it approximated too closely to the wages he would have earned in employment. On the whole, through the '20s, the trend had been in favour of steadily increased assistance, far above anything which had been contemplated on the introduction of the scheme.

These embarrassments were partly solved in 1934 by the Unemployment Act which transferred financial responsibility for the able-bodied unemployed to an Unemployment Assistance Board, thus partly, but by no means wholly, relieving the rates; at the same time the level of contributions was considerably raised. Ironically these changes took place just at the moment when the employment situation was at last recovering, and from that time the Unemployment Fund steadily accumulated a surplus.

National Health Insurance had never suffered from the difficulties of the Unemployment Fund, and remained in respect of contributions and payments substantially as first established. This implied that by 1942 it was completely out of step with the relief available on the unemployment side. The most serious problems in social security were, however, posed by Pensions. Owing to the combined effect of the fall in the birth-rate and the rise in the expectation of life, the pensioner was coming to dominate the demographic scene, while his vote had become a factor which no party could neglect. In the twenty inter-war years, and in a period of falling rather than of rising prices, the charge for pensions had more than quadrupled; and this was only the beginning of what was to be expected.

The Beveridge Report was written in the optimism evoked by the first assurance of ultimate victory in the war; it put forward a bold programme for the total abolition of Want, through a universal system of social insurance, with public assistance reduced to the position of a final net to catch the few remaining hard cases. What was aimed at was effectively a national minimum above the 'subsistence level' as it had been defined in a number of social surveys. (It should be noted that this minimum was susceptible of very varying interpretation, and over the course of time the social investigators have quite noticeably, although perhaps unconsciously, raised their sights.)

The 'Beveridge Plan' thus demanded an entirely new degree of income redistribution, both vertically from the better off (who would be the main contributors) to the poor (who would be the main beneficiaries), and, through the extended maternity benefits and proposed family allowances, horizontally from the small to the large families in each income group. Nevertheless the Plan as put forward in the Report was carefully balanced, and designed to take account of the particular difficulties which had been encountered in the inter-war years. For the first time a comprehensive and integrated social security scheme was to be established, with special benefits at the normal crises of life: birth, marriage and death; disincentives to work arising from prolonged payments of unemployment assistance, were to be guarded against by making payments conditional upon retraining. Finally the menace of the rising pensions charge was to be mitigated, both by postponing the operation of an extended scheme until funds had accumulated, and by giving a bonus on postponed retirement. The proposed contributions were high, even though the Report (very reasonably) assumed a much lower level of unemployment than that of the inter-war period.

The implementation of the spirit, although not of the detail, of the Interdepartmental Committee programme was carried out hurriedly in a series of important Acts in the first flush of victory. We have already observed in Table 3 the change in the structure of the social services which resulted. Virtually all the expenditure proposals were accepted, even more generously than had been recommended (the continued rise in prices made this almost inevitable), but the Beveridge precautions were by no means respected. An increase of pensions was allowed immediately, not after a period, and, it would appear, there was little attempt to estimate in advance the cost of the whole scheme, including the annexed national health service. In one respect the scheme encountered much smoother waters than the Committee had anticipated: with full, and overfull, employment the demands on the unemployment side have so far been negligible. The inflationary pressure of which this is the reflection has however tended to increase the difficulties of other aspects of the scheme.

The establishment of a national health service did not fall within the Beveridge terms of reference, but its existence was assumed in the Report as a necessary move in the campaign against Want. The idea of a universal public health service was not new; it had been mentioned as early as 1920 by the Consultative Committee of the newly reformed Ministry of Health; during the inter-war period the idea was gradually gaining ground and concreteness until it became a definite programme of the British Medical Association in 1938 ('A General Medical Service for the Nation'). The second world war, both by evacuation and by conscription, demonstrated to all how unsatisfactory the health of many still was.

A more unified health policy was clearly called for; health insurance payments, with the rise in prices, were no longer of much use to the sick, while their great weakness was that they covered only the insured worker himself, making no provision for his family. The Local Authorities had inherited in 1929 a motley collection of hospitals from the defunct Poor Law Guardians; the voluntary hospitals were of very differing size and standard, and, save in the large towns, their services were almost completely unco-ordinated. Moreover, and this was the crucial point, their finances were breaking down. On the one hand modern treatment called for unbelievably expensive drugs and apparatus, on the other surtax and death duties were reducing the stream of charity to a trickle. In order to deal with this problem, at the same time as the national health service with free treatment was introduced, the hospitals (both voluntary and local authority) were nationalized under regional boards responsible to the Minister of Health.

The new Health Service came into operation in July 1948; almost at once its finances began to get out of hand. At 100 per cent. subsidization the demand for prescriptions and for treatment (especially for dentures and spectacles) enormously exceeded such vague expectations as had been formed. Total outlay on the service (as appears in Table 3) rapidly climbed to over £400 mn., of which only a very minor part could be covered by insurance contributions. Attempts to contain the flood were made in two directions: ceilings were fitted on to the costs of those parts of the service where they could be made to stick: first on the dentists and then on the general practitioners. On the other side a gradual retreat from the principle of free treatment began. Small charges were made for dentures and spectacles; finally came a general charge for prescriptions (proposed by the Labour Government in 1951 but implemented by the Conservatives). While the initial attempts at ceilings and charges may have been somewhat clumsy, it is clearly necessary in the interests of the service itself, no less than those of a balanced development of the social services, that the finances of the Health Service should be properly controlled.[1]

A more lasting difficulty of the new social security system is the still unsolved problem of the burden

[1] A Committee was set up in the spring of 1953 to examine this question.

of the Pensions charge. As we have seen, contrary to the Beveridge proposals, increased pensions were made available immediately, and with the continued rise in prices it became necessary to raise them more than once. At these high levels the gap between contributions and outlay begins to be serious; it is estimated at £100 mn. in 1957, rising to £200 mn. ten years later, even if no further expansion in benefits takes place.[1] But, ironically the scheme is as far as ever from abolishing Want, in the sense that year by year since its inauguration, increasing numbers of pensioners have needed to apply for, and have received, public assistance; indeed this is the most important cause of the rise in assistance expenditure between 1949 and 1951, shown on Table 3.

Thus the social security programme, which in the 1920s and '30s was mainly devoted to providing a livelihood for the unemployed of working age, in the 1950s was fast becoming a gigantic scheme for supporting the elderly. It would seem that the realization of the Beveridge ideal, if indeed it is practicable, requires either that the elderly work much longer and harder than at present, or that still higher taxation be imposed on those of working age. The seriousness of this alternative will become apparent when we examine the tax structure in the next chapter.

House building by local authorities is from the economic point of view by far the most important social service added to the list within the last generation; though its significance is mainly on investment account,[2] it is apparent from Table 3 that outlay on

[1] See A. T. Peacock: *The Economics of Social Insurance*.
[2] See pp. 65 below.

current account is by no means negligible. On the average, in the inter-war years more than 1 in every 4 houses in England and Wales were built by a local council, while in Scotland, where for a number of reasons building was less attractive to private enterprise than in England, the proportion was still higher.[1] After the end of the second world war the public demand became altogether dominant; on the average of the years 1946–50 between 8 and 9 of every 10 houses erected were built by a public authority, using however for the most part private contract labour. Although there has been from 1951 a slight revival of direct private house building the local councils remain the great providers of new houses.

The causes which led to the establishment of housing as a social service are complicated, and the policy followed at different periods reflects cross currents of opinion. A first interest in the 'Housing of the Working Classes' can be traced from the 1890s, but it was not an interest in good accommodation as such; rather it was what has been called a 'sanitary'[2] policy of clearing the slums, considered as breeding grounds of disease, ignorance and crime. Under this view local authorities were permitted, at their own expense, to pull down slums and to rehouse the inhabitants; the results were the dreary 'tenement' houses prominent in a number of large cities on the eve of the first world war. Only wealthy cities could afford to take action, and that only in a very small way. Until the 1920s there were no local Housing Departments in the modern sense. Although the tenements were built as cheaply as possible, in the absence of a

[1] See M. E. A. Bowley: *Housing and the State.*
[2] See Bowley, *op. cit.*

subsidy, the rents were still out of range of the people for whom they were really intended.

In spite of this unpromising start the 'sanitary' aspect of local housing is of great and continuing importance. In the 1930s legislation was passed which made slum clearance and rehousing (without which clearing one slum merely produces another) much more effective; the experience then gained may be expected to bear fruit when the present phase of new building has passed its peak. The secret of successful slum clearance as discovered in the 1930s seems to be, first, to provide a subsidy which is directly related to the numbers rehoused, thus concentrating attention on the larger families; and secondly to substitute for the vague concept of a 'slum' which must always be a matter of opinion, that of 'overcrowding' which can be objectively measured. Apart from the immediate benefit to slum dwellers, should we ever again need large scale public works to combat unemployment in the constructional industries, slum clearance and rehousing provides an almost perfect answer; by stepping up the criterion of 'overcrowding' new demand is automatically created; economic improvement proceeds *pari passu* with social betterment.

Direct slum clearance however has never played an important part in local authority housing. A positive policy of additional housing emerged from the first world war. In the pre-war decade building costs had been high and the output of houses consequently low; there was thus a back log to make up, even apart from the war years. Further there was a general desire to improve standards, to make 'homes fit for heroes'. At prices of the early 1920s it was certain that these would be beyond the reach of working class families unless heavily subsidized. At the same time the persistence of controlled rents on pre-war small houses made it less likely that private enterprise would again build large numbers of small houses to rent. The immediate answer to these difficulties, it was generally agreed, was subsidized local authority building. After a somewhat slow start, due to inexperience with subsidies on the part of the central government and to dealing with contractors on the part of the local authorities, local authorities worked up to an output of 104,000 houses in 1928, not far short of the 135,000 built in the same year by private enterprise.

This was essentially a short-term policy; there was less general agreement concerning the longer-term place of local housing in the economy; the Labour party viewing subsidized housing as an important new social service, the Conservatives tending to regard subsidies as mainly appropriate to slum clearance and rehousing, the normal provision of new houses being adequately taken care of by private enterprise and unsubsidized local authority building. In the 1930s the turn of events seemed to favour this view. Thanks to the fall in building costs, especially the cost of borrowing,[1] in 1939 local authorities built 100,000 houses without subsidy, while of the 230,000 erected by private enterprise in the same year, a high proportion were of a size which catered roughly for the same income groups. The fact that these were for sale rather than rent was not of first importance, since Building Societies were now prepared to offer mortgages on very favourable terms.

By the end of the second world war however the situation had again drastically changed. Owing to the

[1] See next page.

temporary cessation of new building and to damage by enemy action, the housing situation had once more become serious. Moreover rent control, more rigid and more universal than after the first world war, was preventing the most economic use of existing accommodation. In the longer run it would also give rise to a serious deterioration in its quality, but this was not yet fully apparent.

In these circumstances it was decided by the Labour government to concentrate the whole of the provision of new houses under the local authorities. For this there were plausible economic arguments; scarce supplies could be more easily controlled and allocated to a limited number of local authorities than to a myriad of small private builders. Interest rates, already low, could be made still lower to local authorities, through a new system of re-lending by the Treasury established in 1946.[1] Above all it was clear that by concentrating responsibility in the hands of the local authorities, with their extensive housing estates, opportunity could be taken of still further improving the standard of accommodation and the lay-out of houses. Supplementary to this policy, although it proved far harder to achieve, was the establishment of entirely new towns by public corporations.

The local authorities, now possessing experienced housing departments, for the most part responded enthusiastically to the challenge; moreover with the removal by nationalization of the major local trading services, housing became the most interesting aspect of Council work. Already in 1947 by building 83,600 houses the local authorities had surpassed their pre-war record in all but two peak years; 1948 output

[1] See below p. 128.

more than doubled the 1947 figure. But the 83,000 houses of 1947 had cost £250 mn. as against some £40 mn. for the 100,000 of 1939; and housing costs were continuing to rise. Moreover, building labour, sadly less productive as compared with the 1930s, showed if anything a retrograde trend. In the absence of private building it was only with the most strenuous efforts that the total supply of new housing was brought up to the level of the worst years of the 1930s.

One explanation of the somewhat disappointing results of local authority building between 1945 and 1951 was the larger size and superior amenities provided in council houses. While quality is in itself an excellent thing, when it means slow building the few are benefited out of proportion to the many. Indeed one of the troubles with local authority housing all along has been the tendency to concentrate on the relatively large 'three bedroom parlour house', which fails to take into account the fall in the size of the typical family. Between the censuses of 1931 and 1951 the small family increased substantially at the expense of the larger, while the 'one person' family actually doubled, as compared with an average population growth of only 9 per cent. In 1952, by concentrating on somewhat smaller houses, and by introducing more variety and especially by reducing building delays, a remarkable increase in productivity was brought about. As a result, by 1953 local authority new houses had been stepped up to the unprecedented rate of 300,000 a year, while at the same time some scope had been found for private enterprise.

In a sense this policy was all too successful. In the 1930s besides the social benefits accruing from the provision of more and better houses by local authorities, a direct economic benefit accrued to the under-employed constructional industries; the building boom proved more efficacious than any other factor in sustaining the level of effective demand, and goes far to explain the lesser severity of the slump in this country as compared for instance with the United States.

In the years since 1946 the situation has been exactly the opposite. Housing is directly competitive with other equally important needs; the more materials are used in housing the smaller will be our exports; the more soft wood or other imported materials are used for housing the larger must be our exports. In post-war conditions the social benefits from additional housing need to be weighed carefully in terms of other essential imports such as food and textile fibres, and of alternative uses for housing labour. It cannot lightly be concluded that the more houses the better. With the persistence of rigid rent control, however, the apparent demand for houses remains almost insatiable; until this dilemma has been squarely faced [1] there can be no permanent solution of the housing problem. While some relaxation of rent control would no doubt lead to a temporarily increased demand for building labour, which would have to be met, it seems highly likely that in the longer run we neither need nor can afford to devote so large a proportion of our scarce resources to housing as we have done since 1946.

Food subsidies form the third large field of social outlay which has developed in recent years. Housing benefits the poor differentially more than the Health

[1] A first step is the Housing Repairs and Rents Bill, in course of debate as this goes to press.

service, although the lowest income groups are not always able to afford the rents of council houses, in spite of ever rising subsidies. Food subsidies on the other hand benefit the very poorest more than others, since food is a much more important item in their family budgets than it is further up the income scale. If however the subsidies are freely available to all, the cost of providing this special benefit is (as we have seen) likely to be very high.

The only food subsidies which are now officially regarded as a permanent part of the social programme are those known as the Nutritional Services (see Table 3). These must be regarded as having their origin in the school meals, which, as we have seen, local authorities were empowered to provide from 1907. During the inter-war period an increasing number of local authorities took advantage of this power, and for the most part the tendency was for less and less to be demanded from parents towards covering costs. In the later '30s a service of cheap milk for school children and nursing mothers began, very largely as the result of the excess supplies of liquid milk which the newly established Milk Marketing Board had called forth by its incentive prices to farmers. Behind the new policy, however, lay an impressive amount of biochemical research, emphasizing the nutritional importance of the vitamins in which milk is especially rich.

The real development of the nutritional services took place only during, and largely in consequence of, the war. As a means of ensuring that vitamin products reached those who needed them most, the schools meals service was greatly extended, and payments reduced still further, while cod liver oil, orange juice and other nutritional foods were made available free of cost to children and nursing mothers in their homes. At the present time the outlay of £65 mn. on nutritional foods is divided almost equally between school and home services.

The importance of the nutritional services for the health of the nation can hardly be exaggerated; their success is sufficiently demonstrated by the decline in infant and maternal mortality, and by the greater strength and size of children in all age groups. From the economic point of view these subsidies are also efficient, in the sense that nothing is wasted on those who do not need them. This new service seems to be uniquely developed in Britain; other countries may give more aid to the family by direct cash payments, but while these may be more effective than nutritional subsidies in raising the birth-rate, if such is desired, they do nothing to ensure that the quality of the population will also be improved.

Far more expensive, but much less efficient in operation, were the general food subsidies operated during and immediately after the war as a vast trading service by the Ministry of Food. When these were started they had the double aim first of ensuring (in conjunction with the rationing system) fair shares all round of scarce supplies, and secondly of stabilizing the cost of living. As continued after the war the subsidies retained this latter object but became at the same time more specifically redistributional, aiding differentially, as has been said, the very poor.

The decision to continue the subsidies after the end of the war soon led the government into stormy waters. On the financial side, with the steady rise in world food prices, the cost of the subsidies steadily mounted; the long-term contracts which had been concluded with a number of producing countries served to postpone, but not in the end to mitigate, the effect on British prices of this rise. The devaluation of sterling in the summer of 1949 made the situation still more difficult. Even before that point, however, the government had determined that a ceiling must be fixed to the total outlay on subsidies, at about the level (of £400 mn.) that had then been reached.

It was indeed evident that the cost of the subsidies had got out of line with other expenditure, not excepting other social expenditure. Nevertheless the ceiling had unfortunate effects on the real value of the subsidies by making inevitable a continuation of close rationing. As world food supplies improved it was impossible for Britain to take advantage of the easier situation until months and even years after other countries, who had taken the plunge of reducing their food subsidies and relaxing their rationing systems, were able to improve their standards of nutrition.

Even when this hurdle was surmounted and it became possible to relax rationing and reduce the subsidies to something under £300 mn., another difficulty remained. The policy of guaranteed prices to farmers [1] (adopted because it was held to be more certainly stimulating than other incentives) had the effect of so expanding the output of certain milk and meat products that they could only be disposed of to consumers at highly subsidized prices, and hence in rationed quantities. Thus, for instance, when world supplies of sugar and cheese were already ample Britain alone of Western countries still had to submit to rationing. This dilemma, although quantitatively less important, has a more enduring significance than

[1] See below p. 60.

those posed by war shortages. Since the general food subsidies are awarded equally to all income groups they are as inefficient as the nutritional subsidies are efficient in reaching their aims. It should earnestly be enquired whether more economical methods of helping the very poor and of stirring farmers to productivity cannot be discovered.

As we have already seen, economic expenditure (that is, expenditure designed primarily to raise the national income rather than to redistribute it) ranks only second to social expenditure in the welfare state. Economic expenditure may take the form either of aid to producers in the private sector or of direct operation by public bodies of trading and producing services. The former consists almost wholly of subsidies on current account; but since the latter are normally expected to pay their way they only call upon public funds for purposes of expansion (capital investment). It is this aspect of their activity which we shall specially need to consider. But though this economic investment is the most important part of public fixed capital formation controlled by the central government, it is only a part of public investment. The building of schools, hospitals, public buildings, and above all houses—social investment—is also important; there is finally the question of expenditure on the roads. Since the problems raised in terms of the use of resources are closely similar for all forms of investment in fixed capital it is convenient to consider them together.[1]

Government aid to particular industries, and

[1] See below pp. 63 ff.

especially to farmers, is no new phenomenon of the post-1945 world; but it has expanded considerably since the 1930s, both in amount (even allowing for the fall in the value of money) and also in coverage. In considering this part of public outlay it must especially be borne in mind that actual expenditure may be a very inadequate indication of the extent of assistance given. Many devices can be used to stimulate productivity or to temper the wind of competition: credit facilities, tax concessions, allocations of scarce materials, which do not involve a direct charge on the exchequer. Some, such as tariffs, may even benefit the revenue. In addition to the rise in actual expenditure all these devices have steadily increased since the 1930s; but their origins can usually be traced well back in the inter-war years.

In 1919, as again in 1945, a number of industries found themselves in reconversion difficulties, and a variety of stop-gap help was given. Thus in the early '20s there was a bread subsidy, a coal subsidy, and special aid for shipping. In order to mitigate the effect of the high cost of borrowing (which ranged between 6 per cent. and 7 per cent. in the early '20s), Treasury guarantees on loans were awarded to firms in a variety of industries, especially those concerned with overseas investment. A number of these ventures turned out badly, and the Treasury had to foot the bill; but the total outlay required was not serious.

After the middle '20s most of this reconstruction aid dwindled away, but the position of industry, especially heavy industry, did not become more happy; further help seemed to be called for. The next type of assistance offered took the form of tax concessions: 75 per cent. remission of local rates for industry, and total removal of farm property and land from local taxation came in 1929; while in 1931–2 a general protective tariff was reintroduced. (The last shreds of the eighteenth-century tariff had been torn up in 1860.) Although these concessions were formally undiscriminating, there was never any doubt that they would assist the heavies and agriculture more than others.

From the middle '30s, however, a new type of economic policy began to emerge, which has in fact proved to be the forerunner of post-1945 policy, especially in respect of agriculture. The principle of producers' Marketing Boards for agricultural produce had already been established in 1931; but until these were supported by import restrictions, tariffs and other means of limiting foreign competition, they were, at least in depression conditions, ineffective as an aid to farmers. By 1933 these 'defects' had been remedied, and the Milk Marketing Board in particular was, as we have seen, almost embarrassingly effective in stimulating farm activity. Still more help was demanded however, and towards the end of the pre-war decade the policy of direct out-payments for different agricultural products and operations was set on foot. By 1938 expenditure amounted to £14 mn., of which the chief items were payments for cattle, sugar beet, and milk; cheap fertilisers were also available. (Wheat growing had also been aided for a few years by a levy on milling, but with the rise in the world price of wheat towards the end of the 1930s this assistance had faded out.)

The post-war development of aid to agriculture is shown in Table 4. Its close relationship to the policy evolved in the 1930s is very evident, although the amounts in real terms are larger; the £48 mn. of 1948 would have represented about £20 mn. in 1938 pounds. It would appear, however, that there has been a noticeable shift of emphasis within post-war policy.

TABLE 4

Expenditure in Aid of Agricultural and Industrial Producers
(Calendar Years)   (£mn.)

	1946	1947	1948	1949	1950	1951
Aid to Agriculture						
Acreage Payments .	19	18	19	16	13	2
Fertilizers, etc. .	6	7	11	12	10	5
Miscellaneous [1] .	9	10	18	25	26	31
Total Agriculture	34	35	48	53	49	38
Aid to Industry						
Departmental Trading Losses . .	19	19	17	10	5	6
Utility Cloth . .	8	16	7	..	..	..
Direct Assistance by Ministry of Supply	7	8	7	4	3	5
Fuel Subsidies .	4	7	4	2	1	..
Civil Aviation . .	5	14	11	9	7	5
Total Industry .	43	64	46	25	16	16
Grand Total .	77	99	94	78	65	54

Acreage payments, whose primary aim is the extension of arable, have recently declined relatively to 'miscellaneous outlay', which comprises such diverse activities as grass and ploughing, grass conservation and fertilization, subsidies for hill sheep, attested

[1] For details see below.

cattle, the rearing of calves, farrowing sows;—in short an emphasis on animal husbandry. This change has also been marked by a further step in inducement: from incentive prices to actual guarantees. As we have seen, this change has had awkward repercussions on the food subsidy system, and in the long run may well prove a very expensive method of wringing additional output from our scanty fields. From the farmer's point of view he can now hardly go wrong in trimming his sails to catch a subsidy; whether the soil of our overcrowded islands can produce a commensurate benefit is unfortunately much less certain.

Aid to industry in the post-war years has also represented a further development of ideas evolved in the 1930s. From 1933 a new policy of industrial subsidization had emerged: there were 'scrap and build' subsidies for cotton spinning and tramp shipping, and a grant for civil aviation, but these seldom totalled more than £2 mn. and £5 mn. respectively. In the post-war years direct assistance and guarantees have been given to industries, and even to individual firms, by the Ministry of Supply, the Ministry of Fuel and Power, and the Ministry of Civil Aviation (as appears from the last three items on Table 4); but the sums involved are much larger than anything that was available in the '30s, and the net has been spread much wider. In addition the Ministry of Supply and the Admiralty have sponsored research, at a cost estimated as high as £60 mn., some of which, such as the work of Power Jets Ltd., has been of direct assistance to the national product.[1]

[1] This outlay has also involved a considerable volume of capital formation, see Table 5 below.

The first two items of post-war aid to industry are substantially without precedent in the 1930s, and call for some explanation. Like the Ministry of Food, although on a much smaller scale, the Board of Trade and the Ministry of Supply entered the trading business during the war; for wartime purposes a great simplification was achieved by Ministerial purchase and allocation. After the war these departmental trading activities were also continued, but with a change of emphasis. The departments now became instruments in the policy of stable prices of wage goods and its corollary of income redistribution. In the early postwar years considerable losses were realized on the purchase and re-sale of leather, cotton, wool, and other materials, mainly destined for manufacture into tax free 'utility' goods; direct payments were also made to manufacturers who undertook to obey the utility rules. When it became necessary to impose a ceiling on consumers' subsidies the prices of these goods were gradually eased up to market levels, subsidization being retained only for the basic foods, so that departmental losses substantially declined.

One important material however continued to receive aid after the rest had ceased. This was steel, and the primary object was to keep the price of steel low in the interests of reconstruction, especially house building. In fact, since the demand for steel has a high elasticity, total demand was by this means considerably exaggerated, and hence also the demand for additional steel works, themselves among the greediest consumers of steel. In a world in which steel was already in short supply this policy tended to make it still shorter, and so to delay the necessary industrial reconstruction. This is an interesting example of the way in which a subsidy (or a tax for that matter) designed for one purpose may have repercussions which actually retard its achievement.

A trading activity somewhat similar to these departmental operations was the work of the Raw Cotton Commission, which in 1946 formally superseded the Liverpool Futures market (suspended during the war). In this case the aim was more purely economic; it was hoped that by bulk purchase on the one hand, and the elimination of speculation on the other, substantial economies could be realized. While it would seem that some economies were achieved, especially in the early post-war years, the Commission proved less flexible and less adaptable to the individual needs of producers than the Market had been. Accordingly the Commission's monopoly was abolished in 1952, in favour of direct contact between manufacturers and importers for those producers who desired it. The Commission however continued to cover the risks of all spinners. This halfway house proved impossibly expensive; in the crop year ending in the summer of 1952 losses of £27 mn. were experienced by the Commission. In November 1953 the Government consequently announced the reopening of the Liverpool Futures Market in the spring of 1954 and the winding up of the Commission at the end of the 1954 crop year. The passing of the Commission is to the disadvantage of the smaller spinners who would have to lock up more of their capital in stocks under any other system; but Market trading seems for the majority of firms to combine desirable choice with cover which is considered adequate.

It remains to be seen how effectively the Market can operate under post-war exchange stringency. If it can be successfully resurrected the additional 'invisible exports' of services which are a by-product of its activities will be a welcome support for the British balance of payments.

Expectations of economies to be achieved by bulk purchase and long-term contract were also an important aspect of policy in trading departments concerned with imports, especially the Ministry of Food. The very peculiar supply conditions under which trading was carried on between 1945 and 1952 makes it difficult to say what advantages might normally be expected from such operations. British experience in these years however makes it abundantly clear that in a world of shortages a country with a weak balance of payments and adverse terms of trade is also a weak bargainer. In such a situation any attempt to substitute political pressure for economic bargaining power, as is all too tempting, can have the most disastrous results in the longer term.

Public trading operations of this nature have also another aspect of national importance. By accumulating (or decumulating) stocks the departments are carrying on public investment (or disinvestment) on a large scale. There is of course no inherent objection to this, but unless stock movements are integrated with general fiscal policy they may have the effect of nullifying budgetary effort. The first step towards avoiding this danger is a system of accounts which ensures that a true record of the timing and real value of stock movements is available to the planners. This is a question to which we shall have to return in Chapter V.

Of much greater importance for investment policy

is the acquisition of fixed assets by public authorities. Table 5 attempts to record the development of different types of capital formation in the public sector since 1948, the first year for which official calculations are available, and to compare them with such figures as are available for 1913 and 1938. The figures relate to gross investment, including, that is, the maintenance of assets by replacement; this is advisable, since depreciation calculations are notoriously tricky, especially in times of rapidly changing prices. The use of gross figures however precludes an estimate of the rate at which the public sector is adding to its stock of equipment; but on the other hand it gives a better measure of the demands of the public sector on the services of the constructional industries. To complete this however some further figures of gross output are desirable, and for this purpose outlay on road mainten-ance (which often shades imperceptibly into road improvement) has been added to the table.[1] It must further be remembered that to a considerable extent defence expenditure also makes calls on the construc-tional industries, especially on steel supplies, but it is not possible to make allowance for this.

The first impression created by Table 5 is one of great expansion of public investment in all directions, but, even apart from the effect of the change in the value of money, so that equipment costing £100 in

---

[1] There is also a case for including building repairs on the same argument, but after some hesitation the Central Statistical Office decided not to do this. The question essentially turns on whether we are primarily interested in recording the demand for the products of the investment (or constructional industries); or in distinguishing between outlay reckoned on current and on capital account respec-tively.

TABLE 5

The Structure of Public Capital Formation [1]   (£mn.)

	1913	1938	1948	1949	1950	1951
Post Office, etc.	4	21	37	44	43	51
Other Central Government [2]	..	13	53	59	71	80
Housing	1	67	307	285	282	307
of which: Local	*1*	*67*	*270*	*267*	*266*	*284*
Central (Temporary)	..	..	*28*	*5*	*2*	*1*
New Towns, etc.	..	..	*9*	*13*	*14*	*22*
Education	3	16	24	39	52	64
Other Local Authority [3]	14	95	67	68	84	103
Health Services	1	3	13	16	17	17
National Coal Board	..	..	24	31	28	31
Electricity [4]	2	20	81	125	142	150
Gas [5]	1	2	4	20	35	42
Transport [6]	1	3	51	61	64	60
Airways	..	..	9	13	9	8
Total	27	240	670	761	827	913[7]
Road Maintenance	22	72	74	73	75	74
Grand Total	49	312	744	834	902	987

[1] At Current Market Prices, Gross Fixed Capital Formation.

[2] Including: Raw Cotton Commission, Industrial Rehabilitation, Nutrition Services, Ministry of Supply Research, Central Government Buildings, B.B.C., Road Development and Minor Services.

[3] Including: Water, Sewerage etc., Local Government Buildings, National Assistance, School Meals, Child Care and Minor Trading and other services.

[4] Local Authority until 1948; including also North of Scotland Hydro-electric Board.

[5] Local Authority until 1949.

[6] Local Authority until 1948.

[7] Exclusive of £46 mn. in Iron and Steel.

1948 and £150 in 1951 could be bought for £42 in 1938, on closer examination it will be seen that in several directions the expansion is not great, is even smaller than might reasonably have been expected.

The most obvious case of this is road expenditure; in terms of real maintenance outlay is far below the pre-war level, while development of new roads and major improvements of existing highways [1] has been negligible since 1938, never exceeding £7 mn. in any year. This stagnation is clearly quite inappropriate for the trend of road traffic; it cannot be doubted that it is leading to serious and costly delays in road transport, quite apart from the increased danger of accidents. It was perhaps arguable that, just as road expenditure can most easily and fruitfully be expanded in times of under-employed resources, so the highways can most easily be economized on in times of severe pressure on investible resources; but this argument is hardly applicable in 1953. It seems that we urgently need a new method of measuring our road needs, and in this, as we shall see later, a better system of accounting might play an important part.

Surprisingly enough it will be seen also that the nationalized industries are not great investors, apart from electricity. This is particularly true of the National Coal Board.[2] Even in money terms its figures of gross capital formation were nearly stationary over this period, while if depreciation (on ordinary accounting methods) is deducted, net new investment has in only

[1] Falling on the Road Fund vote in the central government accounts and included with 'other central government' in Table 5.

[2] It must however be remembered that coal mining is a 'labour intense' industry while in electric power production the capital cost per unit of output is exceptionally high.

one year (1949) exceeded £7 mn. This stagnation in coal is the more serious when we consider how basic it is to other industries, both public and private. It is clearly urgent that first attention should be given to opening out whatever bottle-necks (stated to be mainly a shortage of mining engineers) are now retarding the development of coal.[1]

One result of the failure of the supply of coal to expand and consequent rationing of consumption has been an exaggeration of the demand for electricity, especially by domestic consumers. On the supply side, moreover, the practicability of building additional power stations has been exaggerated by the subsidized price of steel; the relatively high rate of capital formation in electricity is thus easily explained, although not necessarily justified. Moreover the demand for power station capacity is governed by peak demand; at present the B.E.A.'s price structure does nothing to induce consumers to economize at peak periods; until this is done demand will continue to be exaggerated and it will remain impossible to determine the appropriate supply capacity.

The most significant item in the whole table however is the preponderance of Housing in the field of public investment in the post-war world. In 1951 house building by public authorities, at £307 mn., made almost as great demands on the constructional industries as the nationalized industries and post office services taken together (£342 mn.). These figures pose in more acute form the question we already asked

[1] The Annual Report of the N.C.B. published in November 1953 showed some improvement in the rate of investment. By 1954 it is hoped to recover to the dimensions of the initial 'Plan for Coal'.

ourselves in relation to current account expenditure: from the longer-term point of view can the country really afford its present outlay on housing?

Investment in housing has another aspect also: it is highly redistributive. If we add to it investment in schools, hospitals and other social purposes, redistributive public capital formation greatly exceeds investment designed to raise the national product. The nationalized industries work ultimately under the direction of their Ministers; we must assume that their performance in some way represents the policy of successive governments. In this case, if the total capital formation in the economy is to be sufficient to enable us to maintain our place in the world economy, it is clearly of great importance that ways of stimulating investment in privately-owned industry should be pressed forward with every possible means, fiscal and other.

Chapter III

THE ADJUSTMENT OF THE
TAX STRUCTURE

THE expansion of public expenditure carries with it a
parallel growth of taxes; but in our period it has
implied something more than a mere quantitative
expansion. Just as the key to the expansion of public
expenditure is the growth of social expenditure, so on
the revenue side the welfare state calls for emphasis
on particular taxes. The changes which have taken
place in the composition of the tax structure are even
more interesting and significant than its quantitative
growth.

Before we set out to examine how the additional
weight has been distributed we must attempt to answer
the simple question: what is a tax? The traditional
definition would run something like this: 'a compulsory
contribution demanded by authorities with tax jurisdiction to defray the cost of the public services'. This will
serve well enough, so long as we are aware of certain
important borderline cases. The most important of
these is the beneficiary's contribution to social security;
this is only partly compulsory in the sense that in the
absence of a state scheme of social insurance most
workers would probably contribute to voluntary schemes
for much the same purposes. For this reason some
people like to regard social insurance benefits as a
right rather than a social service, such as free education
or non-contributory pensions. In fact however their
compulsory nature is an essential element of the

contributions; in its absence sufficient funds for the services would not be forthcoming, and on the other side the contributions made are not closely related to the benefits provided. The biggest difference is in respect of the national health service where no more than one-tenth of total outlay is covered by contributions.

Another important borderline case is concerned with the monopoly profits which might in principle be made by any nationalized industry, but which up to the present have only accrued from the operation of the postal services. If we could isolate the monopoly element in postal charges it would be more accurate to regard only this as tax, in distinction to the return on the capital invested, which would rank as 'income from property'. In fact, however, from the speeches of successive chancellors it is apparent that postal rates are regarded by the government as just a tax which can be manipulated for the same purposes as other taxes on goods and services.

Finally it should be noted that except as regards social insurance, 'authorities with tax jurisdiction' are synonymous with governing bodies: Parliament and the councils of local authorities. Taxing is a political right which cannot be delegated, even to semi-public authorities. The apparent exceptions, such as the charging of water and drainage 'rates' by privately owned public utilities, are more properly regarded as the charging of a fee to cover the services rendered.

We have taken it for granted that a rise in public expenditure must entail a parallel rise in taxes. Only a few years ago this would have been regarded as axiomatic, and it would further have been agreed that virtually the only reason for levying taxes is to raise funds to defray the cost of government. This view reflects two circumstances which no longer hold unequivocally: first that, come what may, good financial habits require the full balancing of expenditure by revenue, and secondly that, by and large, taxes do not have imputable social and economic effects, or at least not of an importance to weigh against the paramount necessity of balancing the budget. We must postpone discussion of the first of these questions to Chapter V, but the second is our present concern.

Probably the only permissible exception to the dictum that the business of taxes is to raise revenue would have been the taxes upon alcohol which from the days of the dreadful 'gin age' in the eighteenth century have been deliberately imposed at penal rates to encourage sobriety, a task which they have performed with such success that they are now a failing source of revenue. Everyone always agreed of course that paying taxes was an unpleasant business and therefore likely to have restrictive effects; on the other hand the Victorians tended to regard taxes as a useful moral discipline in making the taxpayer recognize his responsibilities as a member of the body politic.

The Victorian remedy for the restrictive effect of taxing was to keep down expenditure, effectively to plan the budget on the revenue side, limiting expenditure to what could be covered by acceptable taxes, and especially to avoid those which fell directly on any part of the productive process. In the present age we have discovered so many public wants that budgets tend to be planned on the expenditure side, at least in developed countries, which implies a necessity for tax rates so high that their economic effects can no longer be neglected. Happily, if in one or two instances we can turn these effects to the service of general policy. For the rest, in so far as substantial reduction of taxes rates is unlikely, we must be even more careful than formerly about our choice of taxes.

Further, it has been pointed out that modern governments in developed countries with flexible credit systems do not *need* to levy taxes in order to get command over the resources necessary to finance the public services; they can always borrow, either by raising loans or bills or merely by printing notes. Thus a new way appears to be conjured up of side-tracking the restrictive effects of taxes; this may well be of great importance when the restrictive effects are serious, as in depression; this again is a matter to which we shall have to return in Chapter V. Some of the 'functional finance' group of economists who have put forward this view most strongly go so far as to claim that the primary purpose—or even the sole end—of taxation is to prevent inflation. To the moral argument they would probably reply, and with considerable justice, first that the taxpayer is normally unaware of what taxes he is paying, and secondly that over a large range at least at the lower end of the income scale he is a net recipient of benefits rather than a net contributor to the costs of government.

This way of putting the matter is, however, somewhat misleading, in that in all ordinary circumstances for a government to attempt to cover all its needs by borrowing would be wholly impracticable. We may however draw two important conclusions from this provocative application of modern economic analysis to fiscal policy: (1) that the economically correct amount of revenue to be raised is not automatically given by the expenditure to be financed, and (2) that taxes should be chosen not so much for their formal power of yielding a particular revenue as for their economic and social effects.

The administration of British taxes is somewhat complicated. They may be collected (1) by the central government for its own use, through the Inland Revenue Department or the Department of Customs and Excise (not to mention the Post Office); (2) by the local authorities on behalf of the central government (motor vehicle licences); (3) by the local authorities for their own use (the local rate); and (4) by the Social Insurance Fund for a certain range of defined services only. We evidently need some signposts to enable us to sort out these various tax categories.

The traditional distinction is between direct and indirect taxes, but this on examination proves to be no more than a reflection of the administrative method used. Thus a direct tax is one in which the taxing authority is in direct contact with the taxpayer (or his heirs), as in income tax, death duties, private car licences, and local rates. The indirect tax is one where the revenue authorities approach the taxpayer—say the smoker—indirectly through the manufacturer or wholesaler of the taxed product, who will later recover from the consumer by way of an increased price for the product.

This classification, however, is not economically meaningful because it cuts across more fundamental distinctions. Economically we can most usefully distinguish on the one hand between those taxes which are assessed individually either on the person or the firm according to total income or total wealth (capital)— and in the case of the individual probably also adjusted to take some account of his domestic obligations—and on the other where liability depends only on outlay, or consumption of a particular commodity or service, without reference to general economic position. This gives us a distinction between income and capital taxes on the one hand, outlay taxes on the other. There are indeed important differences between taxes on income and taxes on capital, but since we are here concentrating on their still more important similarities we can neglect them for the present.

The practical difference between the two classifications may not seem on the surface to be very great; by and large direct taxes belong to the income and capital class, indirect taxes to the outlay class. Licence duties on private cars and local rates, however, change over; they are evidently assessed on the consumption of the services of motors and houses respectively and not on the economic position of their owners or occupiers. The vital point is that in choosing a classification that is economically meaningful we can focus attention right from the start on the economic and social effects which we may expect the different taxes to exert.

What part do these two classes of tax play respectively in the British tax structure? Table 6 illustrates the changes in their relative importance which have occurred since 1880. The most striking factor is the steady upward trend in the relative importance of income and capital taxes during the earlier part of the period; since 1933 the trend is less definite, and remarkably, five years after the end of the second war, income and capital taxes were a less important part of the whole structure than they had been five years after the end of the first war.

The short period fluctuations in the relation of the

two sorts of tax are also interesting because they generally reflect policy decisions, sometimes deliberate, sometimes forced on the government of the day by the pressure of events. Thus the expansion in outlay

TABLE 6

The Relative Importance of Income and Capital and Outlay Taxes

(£mn.)   (Selected Years)

Year	Income and Capital	Outlay [1]	Together	Income and Capital as Percentage of Total
1880	9·2	66·4	76·4	13
1885	18·0	87·5	105·5	17
1890	29·3	90·7	120·0	24
1895	30·2	96·8	127·0	23
1905	51·4	114·8	166·0	30
1913	88·0	155·6	243·6	35
1923	440·3	442·3	882·6	49
1933	392·1	485·9	878·0	44
1938	520·3	588·7	1109·0	46
1944	2003·3	1354·2	3357·5	59
1948	1998·4	1964·0	3962·4	50
1950	1994·0	2184·0	4178·0	47

taxes starting in about 1890 was very largely due to the pressure on the local rate as the new elected councils got into their stride. This pressure continued to increase until it was relieved by a substantial growth of exchequer grants shortly before the beginning of the first war; but its later trend is masked by the growth of income taxes and death duties, first in the South

[1] Including Stamp Duties and Local Rates, but excluding Social Insurance Contributions.

African war period and later to finance the new social services.

With the first world war a much greater expansion of income and capital taxes took place, and although the pendulum swung back again when the war was over, largely due to the withdrawal of the excess profits duty, the position gained by income taxes was for the most part held. Before 1913 standard rate did not exceed 1s. 2d. in the pound; in the inter-war years only for one brief period did it fall so low as 4s.; between 1945 and 1950 the minimum was 9s. 6d.

In 1933 the smaller importance of income and capital taxes was mainly due to the depression, outlay taxes being much less sensitive to changes in the national income. By 1938, although the national income had largely recovered, the relative importance of outlay taxes remained high because of the impact of the new tariff imposed in 1932. The expansion of income and capital taxes in the second war again continued in the post-war years; the relative expansion of outlay taxes in the most recent years being partly due to the effect of the repeal of E.P.T. in December 1946 (although much revenue still remained to be assessed and collected), and partly to the growing importance of imports as the empty economies of the world once more returned to normal. Influential also have been a staggering increase in tobacco duties on the one hand and on the other income tax concessions at the lower end of the scale; we shall have to examine these in more detail later.

What, if any, social significance do these changes in the relative importance of the two classes of tax have? Formerly it could be said with conviction that income and capital taxes came from the pockets of the rich, while outlay taxes were paid predominantly by the poor; this is still true in the sense that an overwhelmingly large percentage of income and capital tax revenue comes from those with incomes of £500 or over, while not less than 80 per cent. of the revenue of most outlay tax revenue is derived from those whose incomes are smaller than this; but then 80 per cent. of the population is to be found in these ranges. Since the inclusion, early in the second world war, however, of large numbers of weekly wage earners within the scope of income tax,[1] it is no longer true to say that a reduction of income tax rates is necessarily a present for the rich; on the contrary the concessions granted since 1945 have tended to confer relatively greater benefits on the lower rather than on the higher incomes.

In Victorian times it was also—no doubt correctly in the conditions of the day—argued by economists that income taxes were to be preferred to outlay taxes, not only on distributional grounds, but because they implied no disturbance to consumption or production; income tax could be regarded as equivalent to a lump sum removed from the taxpayer because his only possible reaction would be to substitute leisure for income, and for this he would have no inducement at low rates of tax. The important proviso was, however, always made that rates of tax must not be pushed to the point where the supply of savings for investment would be endangered. It was this fear more than anything else which delayed for decades the intro- duction of progressive rates of income tax; when finally the hurdle was surmounted the supply of savings

[1] In 1938 there were less than 4 million income tax payers, and of these less than a million were weekly wage earners; in 1952 there were over 16 million income tax payers.

seemed to have become so ample that the argument
no longer seemed important. With the very high rates
of profits taxes which have ruled in recent years the
problem has once again attained first importance.

In contrast to the non-substitutability of income
taxes, in respect of almost every commodity which
can be included in an outlay tax there is a possible
substitute, although no doubt less preferred; the
greater the substitution of other commodities in
consumption the higher tax rates must go to bring in
the revenue, and the greater the disturbance to
consumption and production. With current rates of
income tax however the tables seem to be turned:
there is some reason to believe that the heavy smoker
will actually work harder to maintain his consumption
when confronted with a tax-induced rise in prices,
while a great deal of voluntary absenteeism has been
(perhaps not always justly) laid at the door of workers'
income tax. At a later stage we shall have to return to
the examination of these questions.

The main changes which have taken place since
1938 in the revenue derived from the more important
taxes are shown in Table 7. The most striking increases,
it will be easily seen, have taken place in income and
profits taxes, and in the duties on tobacco and alcohol,
while the war baby of purchase tax has quickly gained
full maturity. From a tradition established in 1860
when the final steps to free trade were made, British
taxes on outlay have taken the form of relatively
heavy rates on a limited range of commodities; this
is still largely true. The traditional big outlay taxes
were those on tobacco and alcoholic drinks; today
these are more important than ever. In 1938 the revenue
from tobacco was equal to 1·7 per cent. of the national

income; in 1952 it reached 4·7 per cent. The rise in revenue from drink is less startling; as we have seen

TABLE 7

Major Revenue Sources (£mn.)
(Contributing £50 mn. or more in 1950)
(Financial Years)

	1938	1944	1948	1950	1952
1 Central Taxes					
Income and Capital Taxes					
Income Tax . .	312	1310	1360	1414	1736
Surtax . . .	59	74	100	121	131
Profits Taxes (including N.D.C., E.P.T., Profits Tax and E.P.L.) . . .	15	508	279	268	379
Death Duties . .	78	111	178	186	152
Outlay Taxes					
Tobacco . . .	84	383	604	604	not available
Alcohol . . .	107	356	418	398	,, ,,
Purchase Tax . .	..	98	291	303	,, ,,
Stamps . . .	21	18	57	55	,, ,,
Vehicle Licences .	35	29	53	61	68
Hydrocarbon Oil .	58	57	111	144	not available
Protective Duties .	45	19	46	63	,, ,,
Major Central Tax Sources as Percentage Total Central Taxes .	90%	91%	95%	96%	..
2 Local Rate . .	215	235	319	344	378
3 Social Insurance Contributions . .	109	140	355	443	477

these taxes have shown signs of weakness. Nevertheless revenue in 1952 was equal to 3·1 per cent. of the national income as compared with 2·2 per cent. in 1938.

Apart from convenience in collection there are sound economic arguments for selecting these commodities for relatively heavy taxation. The taxes fall on consumption which does not affect the standard of living of the family, consumption moreover the taxation of which sets up only a weak reaction towards the substitution of other types of expenditure. These taxes thus also approximate to lump sums removed from the taxpayer with a minimum of disturbance to consumption or production. However, as we have seen, this is no longer strictly true of taxes on drink, while the constancy of smokers is partly an illusion due to the still continuing process of the spread of smoking among women; at no distant date this process must come to an end and it may well then appear that the constancy of smokers is not so great as has been thought.

Purchase tax joined the tax structure in 1940. Under certain circumstances a tax covering a wide range of commodities may be preferable to one covering a narrow range. The wider the base of the tax—the larger the consumption taxed—the lower the rates needed to bring in a given revenue. The local rate, which it will be seen, brings in a revenue even larger than purchase tax, is a good example of this principle; there is virtually no family in the country which does not make some contribution to the rate, based on the occupation of house room; but in no case is it a high contribution in relation to family income.[1] For most families it represents but a small fraction of what is cheerfully paid for the pleasures of smoking. These merits of the rate should be borne in mind when we come in the next chapter to appraise the rate critically.

[1] See below p. 134.

Purchase tax with its relatively broad coverage does share some of these merits; but the rates of British purchase tax are far from low: 33 per cent., 66 per cent., and 100 per cent. are indeed fantastically high in relation to its nearest relative, the sales tax of other countries, where rates of 2–5 per cent. are normal and 10 per cent. would be considered extortionate. It was not until the Budget of 1953 that any substantial relief of purchase tax rates was given. The explanation of these high rates has been on the one hand the desire to raise a large revenue (using the tax thus as a controller of consumption), and on the other to exempt from tax the basic purchases of wage-earning households, both on social grounds and as a means of forestalling tax-induced wage demands. In spite, or indeed largely because, of this policy purchase tax bears quite heavily on many household goods whose presence or absence makes an important difference to the comfort of life. It is especially onerous when the commodities in question are effectively consumers' 'capital goods' which will continue to provide services over a period of years. In this case the taxpayer is deprived not only of his present income but also of the interest on it over the lifetime of the goods, so that the rates of tax are even higher than they appear. A further reason for the very high rates of tax on certain articles has been the desire to 'steer' consumption away from them in order to free resources for other purposes. This is a policy which should be used with discretion, as it could easily be abused.

These increases in taxes on outlay since 1938 have been exceptionally heavy. Moreover, as appeared in Table 6, there has in recent years been a shift of emphasis towards them and away from income and

capital taxes. A large part of the explanation of this
has been apprehension of the effects of high income
taxes on the propensity to work, save, and invest. When
we consider the high rates to which the pressure of
expenditure has driven these taxes, it seems only too
likely that these fears may be well grounded. Income
tax is an extremely complicated subject, as can easily
be seen by turning over the pages of the Consolidated
Act of 1951, and we can do no more here than indicate
the places where the shoe pinches worst. The great
importance of income tax, both as a source of revenue
and as a major instrument of income re-distribution,
makes it desirable that we should at least briefly
consider the problems most urgently in need of
solution.

Income tax is the direct descendant of the tax first
imposed by Pitt in the Napoleonic wars and renewed
by Peel in 1842. Until 1910–11 it was imposed at a
single (proportional) rate, but when the rate rose
above 6d. in the pound it was customary to allow a
rebate below the 'standard rate' on small incomes.
The concept of the 'standard rate' is still important
today; it is the rate at which business profits are
taxed and at which tax on dividends is deducted
'at the source'; but so far as personal income tax is
concerned standard rate is just one of a series of
incremental steps of a progressive tax. The steps up
to standard rate are collected as income tax; those
above as surtax.[1] Although undistributed profits only
pay income tax at the standard rate, since 1946 they
have also been subject to Profits Tax (see below); it
will be simpler if to start with we concentrate on the

[1] The name was changed from super- to surtax in the
middle 1920s.

traditional system where income tax alone had to be paid.

In all cases income tax is charged net of the costs of acquiring the income. In the case of personal incomes the costs that are allowed are not very extensive, but they include an allowance for tools and equipment in certain occupations where these are provided by the taxpayer, and, mainly as an encouragement to small savings, insurance premiums and mortgage interest; there are moreover a series of rebates and reliefs designed to fit tax liability to domestic circumstances, especially in the lower income ranges; at a later stage we must examine the extent and significance of these. In respect of impersonal (profit) incomes the question of allowable costs is extremely important, and raises some of the most difficult problems in connexion with the tax; to those we must return in a moment.

At this stage the two most important points to emphasize are, first that British income tax is an interlocked system of both personal and impersonal taxation; secondly that it is a tax solely on net income, and is thus fundamentally different from the gross income taxes and turnover taxes which figure in a number of other tax systems.

The first of these factors has two important consequences: first, within the income tax there is no fundamental difference between the methods of taxation applied to incorporated and non-incorporated businesses respectively. There is thus no fiscal advantage in avoiding incorporation, when a firm reaches a certain size; the result has been that a very large—abnormally large—proportion of British firms are incorporated and are thereby enabled to enjoy the safety of limited liability; this must be counted an important benefit.

Secondly, by the device of taxing at the standard rate in the first instance both personal and impersonal incomes (and later adjusting the former to the global income and personal circumstances of the taxpayer), several important advantages were gained in the traditional system. In the first place income tax is completely neutral as between the allocation of profits to reserves or to distribution; there can be little doubt that this is the right way to start; particular adjustments for the needs of temporary emergencies can be made by other means, as we shall see below. Secondly, tax on property income is collected direct from firms (or in the case of income from rents from the tenants) in a manner which completely prevents evasion. Tax is also collected more speedily than if dividends had first been distributed, although, since the profits assessed are those of the previous year, collection is still not very rapid. Thirdly, there is no double taxation of profits within the income tax, either in the hands of the firm or of the shareholders; it is therefore plain exactly what tax is being paid.

The fact that the tax is assessed strictly on net profits implies that it cannot simply be passed on to consumers in enhanced prices in the manner of an outlay tax;[1] liability to income tax does not determine prices; on the contrary it is determined by the prices which firms obtain for their products. This does not preclude, in certain circumstances where demand exceeds supply and monetary policy permits a continuing price rise, firms attempting a mark-up to cover what they anticipate their income tax liability will be, and actually improving their position by so doing. The conditions for this to work are however exceptional and should

[1] This is equally true of profits tax.

always be curable by other means. There is more justification for the contention that personal income tax may be shifted by demands for higher wages; but again for this to be possible on a large scale we must postulate a certain degree of inflation and over-full employment.

The mixed nature of British income tax implies that it raises two quite separate types of problem, those concerned with the firm and those concerned with the individual. It will be convenient first to examine those connected with the firm. As we have just seen, the British method of taxing firms only through the same medium as individuals had a number of advantages. Unfortunately since 1947 these have largely been sacrificed owing to the imposition of an additional Profits Tax on total net profits before allocation.[1] The profits tax had two parents: the National Defence Contribution, first imposed in 1937 to finance rearmament, and E.P.T. the 100 per cent. excess profits tax of 1939–46, assessed on total net profits in excess of a pre-war standard. The new Profits Tax of 1947 (for it was essentially new, although formally merely a post-war adjustment of N.D.C., a flat-rate tax on industrial profits, imposed at 5 per cent.) had a triple purpose: first to protect the revenue from the loss of E.P.T., secondly on political grounds, mainly as a bargaining counter to secure moderation in wage demands and thirdly, by giving an opportunity for a special discrimination against distributed profits (which as we have seen was not possible within the income

[1] A more detailed analysis would have to include also the various forms of excess profits taxation which have been resorted to: E.P.D. in the first world war, E.P.T. in the second (on these see Hicks and Rostas: *The Taxation of War Wealth*), and also the E.P.L. of 1952.

tax structure), to stimulate real investment by firms.

On the experience of the first world war everyone knew that all sorts of difficulties would arise if E.P.T. were carried on after the end of hostilities; hence there was general agreement when the chancellor (Dalton) announced that E.P.T. would end in December 1946. At that time however E.P.T. was bringing in over £430 mn. a year; it was clear that the revenue could not carry on without some substitute. This situation has endured ever since; indeed revenue from profits tax has risen steadily: £199 mn. in the (financial) year 1948, £258 mn. in 1950, £376 mn. in 1952; we seem to be no nearer being able to do without profits tax than we were in 1946. Yet the economic case for the taxation of reserves is not a good one; it tends to be a tax on productivity of just the sort that the Victorians so carefully avoided.

High taxation of profits may react unfavourably on production in two quite separate ways. In the first place, for an investment to be undertaken, the anticipated rate of return must be high enough to give after tax a net yield which is considered satisfactory. If the rate of tax is high the number of investments carrying such a prospect is inevitably reduced; in fact as the rate of tax rises the pre-tax rate of return which will be required to give a satisfactory post-tax yield rises more than proportionately to the rise in tax rates. Secondly, if rates of tax are high safer investments will be preferred to more adventurous, even though the expected yield is smaller. The (small) chance of a very high gain which would normally make the 'risky' investment attractive is more than offset by the tax which will have to be paid if the project succeeds, while there will be no compensation for loss of capital if it should fail. High profits taxes thus discriminate against 'venture' capital, so necessary to raise the level of productivity. When therefore it becomes possible to relax the need for revenue, on economic grounds a reduction in the taxation of profits should have a high priority. There are really no social arguments against this since social ends can be better served by the progressive taxation of personal incomes.

An important object of the profits tax, however, was the stimulus to investment to be induced by a heavy discrimination in favour of retained profits. This was obtained by charging all profits at a fixed rate and granting 'non-distributional relief' on the retained portion. As time passed the differential became very large: in 1951 with tax at 50 per cent. non-distributional relief amounted to 40 per cent. While at first sight this appears to be an admirable idea, differential rates lead to a most unfortunate complication which becomes cumulative with the passage of time. This works as follows: in a year in which less than total net profits is distributed, non-distributional relief is, as we have seen, available on the part not distributed; but in a year in which more than total net profits is distributed (as is often desirable in the interests of dividend stabilization), the revenue must make a compensating charge representing the distributed rate of tax which would have been paid if the profits had been distributed currently, otherwise the higher rate of tax could be perpetually avoided.

It follows that in every year in which a firm distributes less than its total net profits it is accumulating a liability to 'distributional charge'; over the course of time this liability could reach terrifying dimensions.

This difficulty is inherent in any profits tax which attempts discrimination between distributions and reserves, and hence the principle is not suitable for incorporation in a permanent tax; but the present profits tax has a number of other anomalies amounting to different treatment of different types of business. The neatest way to get out of the dilemma in which we now find ourselves would seem to be to abolish the present profits tax and raise the standard rate of income tax to a point where serious loss of revenue would be avoided. If this produced a personal tax which was undesirably high it could be mitigated by some extension of the relief system, which we shall examine below.

But what of the stimulus to investment to be given by the low taxation of reserves in the profits tax? In the first place it should be noted that the stimulus is directed to the accumulation of reserves rather than to capital formation; but this is perhaps not too important; firms are more likely to invest if they are in a liquid position. Secondly and much more important however, is the fact that in the meantime and by quite an independent route, an important new method has been discovered not merely of stimulating capital formation but of varying the tempo of investment, so desirable in the interests of economic stability. This has come about through the right (first awarded in 1946) to draw in the initial year of the installation of new equipment a more than pro rata percentage of the total replacement (or depreciation) allowance permitted over the life of the asset.

To begin with this 'initial allowance' was fixed at 20 per cent. of the total; in 1948 the figure was raised to 40 per cent.; in 1952 the privilege was withdrawn to set free resources for re-armament; in 1953 it was restored at the 20 per cent.[1] level. The net effect of these variations in the timing of depreciation allowances is not an increase in the total, except in so far as the acceleration implies an interest-free loan from the government to the firm; but if a firm is undertaking a big programme of investment the result will be to reduce substantially current liability to income tax, or even to postpone it indefinitely. Experience so far gathered suggests that firms are extremely sensitive to variations in initial allowances; so that there is reason to hope that a new governor of the rate of investment has been discovered.

In the reconstruction period this device also served another end. When firms came to replace pre-war equipment at post-war prices they found of course that pre-war depreciation allowances were far from sufficient to cover the cost of new equipment. There was an immediate demand that depreciation allowances should be based not on the original cost of the asset but on the current replacement cost. Coupled however with a certain willingness of the Inland Revenue to sanction minor re-equipment as (tax free) running repairs, it is estimated that the existence of the initial allowance privilege has roughly given firms what they would have had on a replacement-cost basis. Although it worked, this is not necessarily a good solution of the problem of the inadequacy of depreciation allowances based on original cost; but this is not a continuing problem and only becomes of major importance as a result of a great and rapid rise in prices.

[1] Or more precisely 10 per cent. for industrial buildings, 20 per cent. for plant and machinery, and 40 per cent. for mining works.

Impersonal income tax is concerned with the willingness and ability of firms to save and invest; important as this is, over 60 per cent. of income tax revenue (including that of the profits tax) is derived from personal taxation. Hence in many respects the more serious problems are concerned with the effects of taxation on individual willingness to work, and to save.

In respect of personal incomes, as has been said, income and surtax are assessed in a series of incremental or 'marginal' steps; the standard rate is the fifth of these steps and it is followed by eleven steps of surtax. These are shown in the 'marginal rate' line of Chart II. The corresponding 'effective rate' (total tax paid divided by total income) is shown as a continuous wavy line on the same Chart. Two pairs of curves are shown: A and A' relating to a single taxpayer with all investment income, B and B' relating to a married couple with three dependent children, where the whole income is derived from work. The marginal curves coincide from £2000. The steepest parts of the curves occur first, where liability to income tax begins, and secondly where liability to surtax begins. The flattest part is found in the highest ranges because tax liability approaches so close to total income that rates cannot be much further increased.

Tax as we have seen is assessed on income net of allowable costs; but in this connection there are three points to notice: first the incomes of husband and wife are aggregated for assessment, secondly an imputed income for a house owned and occupied is included in taxable income, but not an imputed income for any other capital asset; thirdly, and this is especially important, taxable income is defined as a stream of payments. Capital gains are hence tax free, although if

CHART II. THE STRUCTURE OF INCOME TAX

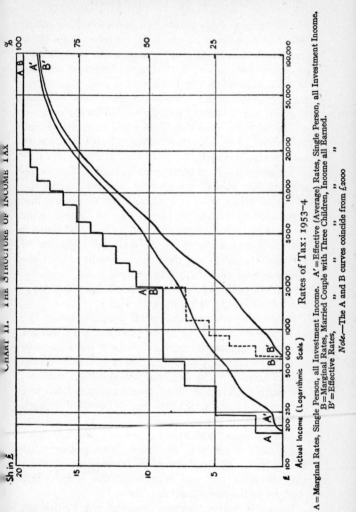

Rates of Tax: 1953-4

A = Marginal Rates, Single Person, all Investment Income. A' = Effective (Average) Rates, Single Person, all Investment Income,
B = Marginal Rates, Married Couple with Three Children, Income all Earned.
B' = Effective Rates, " " " " "

Note.—The A and B curves coincide from £2000

the taxpayer makes a habit of buying and selling assets, either as a business or as a hobby, his gains are liable to be included in his taxable income. In the case of a small company where the managers might be tempted to avoid their surtax by retaining unemployed reserves and later distributing them as tax-free capital bonuses, funds in excess of those actually needed for the business are liable to be treated as if they had been distributed and added to the directors' surtax in accordance with their several interests.

These methods of countering evasion of surtax by substituting capital for income receipts should be borne in mind when we come later to discuss the suggestion that we also need a tax on capital gains *per se*. Although they are effective it cannot be claimed that they completely check evasion; the ingenuity of lawyers is infinite; and there is always the case of the taxpayer who speculates frequently but not regularly. Over him the Inland Revenue must use their discretion; but fortunately he is a fairly rare bird.

Progressive taxes are in general now assessed on the incremental method; in broad outline the British tax is very similar to the personal income taxes in force in the Dominions, the United States and the Scandinavian countries. In one way or another, however, the British tax tends to be tougher (apart from any difference of rates, which also tend to be rather higher). In addition to the inclusion of the imputed income from the home, which is exceptional, and the joint assessment of husband and wife, there is very little flexibility in the treatment of fluctuating incomes, and that little confined to authors; this is in strong contrast to the Scandinavian taxes.

In one important feature, however, the British tax

is uniquely generous: in the reliefs and allowances given, on the one hand on income that is earned, on the other to take account of the taxpayer's domestic circumstances. The first was originally intended as a recognition of the fact that income from property is more certain and enduring than income from work; more recently it has been used as an incentive; [1] with this end in view it has been raised several times since 1945. The second group in effect date from the end of the first world war and are primarily social in purpose. As will be seen from the two curves of effective rates in Chart II the operation of the reliefs makes a substantial difference to tax liability. The earned income relief and the personal allowance for age (where income does not exceed £600) are given in the form of a percentage deduction (at present two-ninths) from marginal rates (so that a marginal rate of 3s. in the pound becomes 2s. 3½d.); the other personal reliefs (for self, wife, dependent children, and so on) are given in the form of flat sums, which consequently affect only average liability, so that an increase of them is less stimulating to the taxpayer. Since the earned income relief has a 'ceiling' (of tax on £450), the effect of the reliefs gradually declines as we move up the income scale. In the lower ranges, however, they impart a substantial element of progression to the tax, over and above that afforded by the incremental marginal rates. No reliefs are available within surtax, hence the coincidence of the marginal curves from £2000.

The economic effects of personal income tax impinge both on the willingness to save and the incentive to work. The Victorians, as we have seen,

[1] See also below p. 103.

were particularly anxious to keep income tax low because they relied on personal savings as the chief source for increasing capital formation—savings which would either be lent on the stock exchange or directly invested in the family firm, then the typical form of business organization. This economic set-up has long passed away; early in the inter-war period it was remarked that the main source of savings had become the undistributed profits of firms. This phenomenon was by no means confined to Britain but was equally observed for instance in Canada and the United States where income tax rates were then low. Of recent years in Britain personal savings have become negligible. This is to be regretted since personal savings automatically set free resources which can be used for capital formation in either the public or the private sectors; while if directly applied they might still prove an important source of venture capital.

There is no doubt that in the welfare state both the opportunities and the incentives for saving are much reduced. Yet it is not impossible that tax adjustments might still cause some recovery. In particular the very high rates of surtax and of death duties in recent years (reaching 80 per cent. on the largest estates) have led to a certain amount of dis-saving which largely negatives such savings as are made; in an inflationary situation it also makes consumer spending harder to control by normal fiscal means. This is a point to which we shall have to return later. It may well be, however, that the very low rate of return on lending which ruled from 1945 to 1951 was as great a deterrent to saving as fiscal burdens; in that case we should see some automatic recovery.

Of potentially greater importance than the disappearance of net personal saving is the possibility that high rates of income tax may provide an excuse for substituting leisure for work; this possibility is largely concerned with the effects of the P.A.Y.E. system of current withholding of tax on wage and salary incomes; it is especially important in the lower ranges of taxable income, where as we have seen progression is abnormally steep. To appreciate this we must briefly examine the working of P.A.Y.E.

P.A.Y.E. is based for every pay period on average liability for the financial year up to the date in question, taking account of the reliefs to which the taxpayer is entitled, and also any small additional income he may have from investments or house property. The personal reliefs are treated as accruing evenly through the year at the rate of one fifty-second per week, cumulatively. (Incidentally this implies that the employer has to use a different tax table each week to calculate the proper deductions.) By this means the taxpayer is kept in equilibrium with the revenue week by week; at the end of the year in all ordinary circumstances he will owe the revenue nothing and be owed nothing.

The P.A.Y.E. system is thus extremely equitable, both in the sense of justice between the revenue authorities and the taxpayer, and of justice between the taxpayer whose income fluctuates from week to week and the taxpayer who receives his at a steady rate; but it implies that in every week in which earnings are above the average extra effort will immediately be burdened with extra liability; while in every week in which earnings are less than the average the taxpayer will have overpaid tax on the annual basis, and may not have received his quota of reliefs. In this case the reliefs will be honoured by repayment of tax until the correct yearly rate is reached again. This constitutes a species of 'holiday with pay', which may reach large dimensions if work ceases well on in the financial year.

The problem for the economist and administrator is to determine the importance of the disincentive effect of this device. From the nature of the case it cannot be measured statistically, although there is no lack of casual evidence of substantiated cases where the operation of P.A.Y.E. has been taken into account by the worker to the detriment of his output. Immediately after the end of the war the propensity to work was abnormally low both on account of war-weariness and because war earnings had provided more than ample cash balances to satisfy all needs for the limited range of goods available. When it is a question of accepting or refusing overtime, incentive is probably more directly affected than when it is a question of working normal hours, or indulging in absenteeism with its risk of being fired. In general also the opportunities which many workers have of varying their incomes by varying their efforts are not very great. Nevertheless it remains true that the close tie-up between marginal effort and tax increment which is the peculiar feature of P.A.Y.E. is dangerous, and should be avoided if possible.

The experience of other countries now provides a variety of methods of current withholding from weekly wage earners. In America for instance the basis of assessment remains the year (this is necessary for equity between steady and fluctuating incomes), but the taxpayer is not brought into equilibrium with the revenue until the end of the year, when he normally receives a bonus of overpaid tax—a species of involuntary saving which he apparently enjoys. In principle the simplest substitute method would be to adopt a plain percentage tax for all incomes without exemption up to a point covering the majority of weekly wage earners; the reliefs could be 'coded into' this as percentage deductions. This would eliminate all disincentives due to the difference between incremental and effective rates; the last hour worked would bear the same rate of tax as the first.

It is tempting to look for simplifications because superficially nothing could exceed the complications of P.A.Y.E. As we have seen different tables are required for each week of the year; 183 different codes record not only the taxpayer's right to reliefs, but also 'code in' minor additional income receipts, such as interest on government securities or house rents. These complications lead to a certain rigidity in the tax; it takes about four months for a change in tax rates to become operative in P.A.Y.E.—but then changes in rates cause complications in most with-holding systems. Apart from the fact that much of the work of collection is carried out by firms (although by now businesses of any size have installed machines which perform the calculations), in practice the multi-plication of codes is a great simplification and economy. They obviate the need for getting returns from many millions of taxpayers. Important vested interests have thus been built up in the path of reform, both on the side of the revenue authorities and of the workers.

As we saw earlier, in the modern economy taxes are not merely expected to bring in revenue; they have frequently other jobs to perform. Among the most important of these of recent years has been the promotion of economic stability by controlling in-flationary pressure. One of the most useful aspects of fiscal stabilization is the collection of tax *pari passu* with changes in incomes, thus claiming the revenue's share in expansion before it can be spent, and going soft on the taxpayer when his income is falling. This is an important aspect of all British income tax collected at the source, especially P.A.Y.E., and also of profits tax, which is due one month after the close of the firm's accounting period. Moreover, income taxes which do not lead to a substitution of leisure for effort (and this may well be the typical case) are themselves good stabilizers; while profits taxes which can be combined with a flexible variation in depreciation allowances seem, as we have seen, to be an effective regulator of the tempo of investment.

Even better as stabilizers, however, are outlay taxes which do not lead to a fall in consumption of the taxed article (such as tobacco taxes). There is less certainty, however, that their removal would stimulate the right sort of consumption if unemployment threatened. For a means which could be used as a stabilizer in either direction the variation of social security contributions (officially blessed by the National Government in 1944) would now prove more useful than formerly owing to the greater coverage of the system. In depression conditions, however, it is probable that the best stabilizers are to be found on the expenditure side, including subsidies on consumption, which are in principle negative outlay taxes.

Taxes which lead to additional wage demands or to spending out of capital are obviously not good stabilizers (but as we have suggested it is often other than fiscal factors which are at fault); taxes which discourage people from doing as much or as good work as they could, make everybody poorer than they need be. It cannot reasonably be claimed that our tax system is blameless in these respects, although it is a high tribute both to the taxpayers and to the administration that such a massive revenue can be collected with so relatively little disturbance and inequity. It would take us too far afield to examine in detail the possible alternatives, but three suggestions in particular have received so much publicity that they call for brief mention.

In the first place it is contended that an income tax assessed on some other basis than actual receipts would be less disincentive; it could most plausibly take the form of an annual 'capital' or general property tax, such as has long been traditional in some of the American states and is used in Scandinavia. Secondly it is suggested that capital gains should all be taxed, most plausibly within the framework of income tax; and thirdly, and most logically of all, that a general expenditure tax should be substituted for income tax. This would differ from even the most comprehensive sales tax in having a wider coverage and in being assessed on outlay cumulatively over the year, at rates which would be progressive on the total. In principle each of these would have some advantages over our present tax system; in fact, however, there are weighty difficulties attached to them all.

The annual capital tax presents difficulties of valuation which are not encountered in death duties, because the latter requires no more than a once-for-all assessment; there is no problem of keeping valuations up to date. If the rates of the annual capital tax are kept low and the progression moderate these difficulties do not appear important, but then not much revenue is to be gathered, and as Scandinavian experience shows, the capital tax is not of much use as a stabilizer. It seems probable that the most important use of this tax is as an alternative to income tax on small unincorporated firms who do not keep proper accounts, but, as we have seen, in Britain they are probably a less important element in the economy than in almost any other country.

The taxation of capital gains has an obvious attraction as an instrument against surtax evasion which at present slips through the net; it might also be of some use as a stabilizer. It is notable, however, that it has not yet been achieved in any country without causing very great inequities and anomalies. Two special difficulties have been very generally encountered. In the first place it is felt to be unfair to treat all capital gains as exactly on all fours with the rest of the income stream, since many of them are unwanted or accidental, such as those arising from distress or forced sales. These are especially likely to occur in inflationary conditions when many of the so-called gains are merely on paper; the real value of the assets may even have fallen. Secondly it has been found impossible to treat losses symmetrically with gains because of the ease with which artificial losses can be used to offset taxable income. For this reason rates of capital gains taxes have usually been substantially lower than the upper surtax rates, so that some incentive for substituting capital gains for the income stream still exists, perhaps even a greater incentive than under the British system with its tough treatment of such engineered gains.

In principle the expenditure tax would be ideal in inflationary conditions, penalizing those who by their consumption make calls on the national provision of goods and services and rewarding those who refrain from doing so, in a way which an income tax so lamentably fails to do. In depression it may be supposed that a remission of tax rates would provide an ideal all-round stimulus to consumption. Administratively, however, a general expenditure tax is quite untried, and it cannot be supposed that avenues of evasion would not fairly easily be discovered, by substituting other means of acquisition for purchases. Assessment would have to be on the basis of changes in bank balances, and this would surely give rise to great difficulties in the income ranges which do not normally keep bank accounts.

In practice it would seem that the expenditure tax would approximate to an income tax with larger exemptions than at present for defined methods of saving. There would be a further difficulty in allowing for 'distress' and abnormal expenditure, such as that incidental to illness or even moving house. Exemption could be extended to cover defined types of outlay of this nature, and indeed it would have to be if tax bankruptcies were to be avoided. But any scheme of exemptions would have to be very rigid, so that it would be bound to leave hard cases uncatered for. It is difficult to believe that a tax which was liable to hit people hardest just when they were in difficulties would satisfy the ordinary man's sense of justice.

It would therefore seem as if there were no easy way out of our dilemmas; and there is some reason to fear that in exorcising the devil we know (and of which the revenue authorities largely have the measure) we may be admitting a worse one. A surer policy would concentrate first on improving the black spots in our existing taxes.

It remains for us to examine more closely the

incidence of these taxes, taken together, on different classes of taxpayers. Table 8 allocates total revenue collected according to type and use: personal, non-personal, capital formation, public authorities, and

TABLE 8

The Allocation of Taxes between Consumption and Other Purposes

(£mn.)   (Selected Calendar Years)

	1947	1949	1951
1 *Income Taxes*			
Personal	999	1048	1184
Non-personal . . .	494	733	695
Social Insurance . .	232	436	452
Total Income Taxes .	1725	2217	2331
2 *Outlay Taxes* falling on:			
Personal Consumption .	1648	1829	2014
Less Subsidies . . .	- 441	- 497	- 455
Net Personal Consumption .	1207	1332	1559
Public Authorities . .	40	37	59
Gross Domestic Capital Formation	56	63	100
Exports	27	40	81
Total Net Outlay Taxes .	1330	1472	1799

exports. We can neglect the taxes paid by one public authority to another; they are only a book-keeping transaction. In this period it would not be unreasonable to regard the taxes on exports as paid by foreigners. This leaves to be considered the taxes paid by firms on current profits and on capital formation, on the one hand, and on the other taxes paid by persons and falling on family consumption. Perhaps the most striking feature of the table is the increase in taxes paid by firms since 1947. Much of the taxes on undistributed profits as well as the £100 mn. in taxes on outlay must impinge on capital formation; this underlines the plea we made earlier for a remission of taxes on production.

From the point of view of social policy the personal taxes are the centre of interest. The income distribution of income taxes is already apparent in principle from Chart II, although naturally individual 'effective' curves may take up a variety of patterns. If we were to compare the curves shown in Chart II with the pre-war situation we should notice several important differences: (1) the highest effective rate in 1938 was 65 per cent. of taxable income; for 1953–4 it will be 87 per cent.; (2) as a result of the increase in the value of the personal reliefs the effective rates in general have moved further away from their corresponding marginal curves than was the case before the war; (3) owing to the increase in the earned income relief, the difference between earned and unearned rates has been increased and (on the effective curves) exerts some little influence up to a high level.

We have already seen that an identical percentage relief is available to the elderly whose incomes do not exceed £600, whether earned or not. While this provision may have been introduced with some idea of increasing the incentive for pensioners to continue working, the main purpose was the economy of cutting out of income tax a large number of small incomes which could no longer be reached by P.A.Y.E. In 1952 a significant further step in the same direction was taken by granting the 'earned' income relief to small property incomes, up to tax on £250. (This accounts for the sudden kink at the lower end of the property income effective curve in Chart II.) It seems that the 'earned' income relief is ceasing to be regarded as primarily a compensation for the uncertainty of earnings or as an incentive to increased exertion, and is becoming just one more means of redistributing incomes.

To this account must also be added the effect of death duties. Writers in the first quarter of the century (especially Dr. Dalton in *The Inequality of Incomes*) emphasized that the main cause of continued inequality was inequality in inherited wealth. Even up to the second world war laments were frequently heard that although progressive death duties had been in force since 1894 they had made little difference to the distribution of property. This is no longer the case; with effective rates of death duty reaching to 80 per cent. on the whole estate, without rebate for consanguinity in the heirs, there is no doubt that the break-up of large estates is now taking place rapidly. In addition to gifts *inter vivos* and to capital consumption during life (both stimulated by the prospect of death duties), it is usual for the testator to avoid leaving a large part of an estate to the same legatee: 30 per cent. for the largest bequest is common and on the larger estates it is often considerably less. When these ultra high rates have been in force for some time the effectiveness of death duties in redistributing wealth and income will become obvious—perhaps painfully obvious—to all. Finally it is also worth noting that death duties have recently become more redistributive in the sense that the emphasis has been shifted off the smaller estates; up to 1946 the exemption limit was £100; it is now £2000.

There are as yet no comprehensive estimates available of the income distribution of outlay taxes in the post-war situation. On the basis of extensive pre-war calculations, however, it is possible to estimate their general effect. Taking all the outlay taxes together, in the 1937 situation about 17 per cent. of income on the average went on paying outlay taxes in the range up to £250; at £500 the proportion was about 14 per cent.; from that point it fell steadily, reaching 2 per cent. or less at £20,000. This average expenditure however concealed very large variations in the consumption of certain taxed commodities within income groups; this was especially true of the taxes on smoking and drinking, which, as we have seen, are the big revenue producers. For the abstemious family the proportion of income paid in outlay taxes, even in the lower ranges, would not have exceeded 12 per cent.

In the post-war situation this general pattern no doubt remains, but it has been modified in three respects. In the first place the total tax bill is higher; income for income, on the average about 60 per cent. more than pre-war is paid in outlay taxes. This increase, however, is not distributed entirely on the pre-war pattern; there has been a relative expansion of the taxes with a relatively progressive income distribution, such as motoring duties (which in 1937 were estimated to come equally from the pockets of the under and over '£500s'), and above all in purchase tax, which, owing to the exemption of the lower priced goods, must have a roughly similar income distribution. Thirdly the 'optional' taxes which the abstemious family need not pay now provide over 70 per cent. of the revenue from outlay taxes as compared with only 30 per cent. in 1937. Taking into account the

H

effect of the subsidies on outlay, 80 per cent. of which are due to food, and which, as we have seen, benefit the very poor especially, in 1951 the abstemious family in the lower income groups probably paid less rather than more of its income in outlay taxes than in 1938.

Over and above the redistribution of income through taxation (positive and negative) is the effect of the £1500 mn. social service expenditure (three times as large as in 1937); almost the whole of this accrues to the lower income groups. Whatever the exact balance on the average of the lower income groups may be, we can be pretty certain that they make no *nett* contribution to the enormously increased tax bill of recent years. Rough as these figures are, they serve to define the order of magnitude of the income redistribution through public finance in the post-war world. This is assuredly the leading characteristic of the welfare state.

Chapter IV

LOCAL GOVERNMENT IN THE FISCAL SYSTEM

BRITAIN must be accounted lucky in that she has inherited from the past a strong tradition of local government activity and interest. Like the Scandinavian countries, with which she has in other respects also so much in common, her democracy started at the local end—in the parish and the borough. Indeed it is in the smaller units of government that the virtues, if also sometimes the faults, of democracy have been most apparent. The connexion between the citizens, their elected representatives, and their administrators on the one hand, and the realization of the necessity for paying taxes in order that communal wants may be satisfied on the other, have always been clearest at the local level. Until well into the nineteenth century the combined outlay of the local authorities actually exceeded that of the central government; as late as 1908 the revenue from the local rate amounted to nearly 60 per cent. of central tax revenue.

Notwithstanding the activities of progressive town councils from the mid-nineteenth century, the modern development of local government may be said to date from the establishment of the multi-purpose elected councils established over the years 1888 to 1894,[1] which gradually took over the functions formerly exercised by the justices and a number of ad hoc boards, greatly extending and adding to them. In

[1] See above pp. 3 ff.

1890 at the beginning of this process (as we have seen) local expenditure amounted to over 45 per cent. of total public outlay; with the development of local social and trading services the local share in the public sector steadily expanded, apart from the brief episode of the South African war. In 1905 the local authorities were spending 55 per cent. of public money. From about 1910, however, the position was gradually reversed; the new social services established by the Liberal government were national in scope, control, and finance. By taking the unemployed, the elderly, and the sick partly out of poor relief, and by increasing the importance of grants from the exchequer, the local element in the public sector was substantially reduced, and it never again reached 50 per cent.

After the first world war, and largely as a consequence of it, national expenditure increased so much that the local element shrank to about 35 per cent., exceptionally rising to 40 per cent. during the depression of the early '30s, because of the combined effect of expanded poor relief and of economies at the centre. With the second world war the place of local government in the fiscal system substantially declined; in the late '40s local expenditure did not average more than about 25 per cent. of total public outlay on current account. From this position there can be no great return; the local authorities have lost too much in poor relief, health services, and especially by the nationalization of their most important trading services. Thus from 1910 there has been a steady decline in the demands on the resources of the nation coming from the local side. The decline, however, has not been regular. On the one hand, the Treasury, recurrently apprehensive of the state of national finances, has from time to time sought to limit its own responsibility by putting more on the local authorities; on the other, new local services have arisen to take the place of those coming to an end through nationalization. On the whole, however, the trend has been definitely and significantly downward so far as local government is concerned; the situation which we now have to analyse is thus one implying a substantial break with the old tradition.

The relative decline in the scope of local government does not necessarily imply a parallel loss of local autonomy; even when some services are transferred to national control it is possible that the local authorities should continue as independent as before in respect of those remaining or of any new ones which they may acquire. There is, however, a presumption that a narrower scope of activities carries with it a decline in independence. When we look at the revenue side this presumption is very strongly confirmed.

The traditional local tax, the rate, like the traditions of local government, takes shape gradually out of the mists of medieval public finance. At first used intermittently for particular local needs, such as bridge building or church repairs, the rate became regular and universal under the Elizabethan Poor Law. At about the same time its essential character was fixed by legal decision: that it is to be assessed separately on each 'hereditament' of land and the buildings upon it and that liability depends on occupation, rather than on ownership—at least south of the Tweed. The traditional principle was that a separate rate would be levied in respect of each service, according to its requirements, thus (and this is fundamental for the success of local government) establishing in the minds

of the ratepayers a link between a particular work or
service (whether locally desired or imposed by higher
authority) and the necessity to dig into their pockets
for the necessary finance. The ad hoc authorities of the
nineteenth century, succeeding to this tradition, levied
rates simply for their own purposes; but the poor rate
and the valuation on which it was based gradually
became the nucleus for a combined system of local
taxation covering all services. In course of time (but
not until 1925 outside London) the chaos of separate
rates was consolidated into a single demand note on
which were set out the separate purposes and the rate
required for each.

British local government in this way grew up with a
high degree of administrative autonomy; but it must
always be borne in mind that local councils are
'statutory authorities',[1] creatures of the legislature.
They cannot undertake services without legislative
authorization, and although additional powers have not
infrequently been acquired by the promotion of
private bills, the limits of 'ultra vires', beyond which
they may not stray have always been strictly enforced.
The reverse of this is that local authorities can be
compelled to develop whatever services Parliament may
call upon them to undertake, without legal obligation
on the part of the central government to make special
financial provision. There can thus never be any
question of failure to introduce a service which Parliament is determined to have. This indeed constitutes the
fundamental difference between inter-governmental
relations in a unitary country and in a federation;
in all other respects the problems are closely
parallel.

[1] This is not strictly true of borough councils.

The administrative autonomy of British local government was traditionally accompanied by a high degree of financial independence. The local rate was an extremely powerful tax, the revenue from which far exceeded that of any national government source: customs, excise or (from 1842) income tax. In addition to the rate, at the beginning of our period local authorities were drawing substantial revenue from their rapidly developing trading services: gas, trams, and electricity. (On this there was later a change in policy.)

From this administrative and financial independence there had grown up a distinction which was considered (and was in fact in the circumstances of the time) fundamental, between activities of local interest which were considered 'beneficial' and would naturally be financed wholly from local resources, and activities of primarily national interest which were regarded as 'onerous' from the local point of view, and in respect of which it was consequently reasonable to demand that the exchequer should make some contribution. Services falling into this latter class were especially police, justice, and education. The position of poor relief was somewhat anomalous; at least from the 1870s the central government had tacitly acknowledged that poverty (and unemployment) was of more than local significance, but in the interests of economy any grant aid for this service was steadily refused. As Goschen (one of the most sympathetic of Ministers to local problems) candidly put it, he would not 'open the floodgates on the Consolidated Fund'.

The recurrent burden of poor relief on local finances could thus only be modified as the poor law was gradually 'broken up', and its constituent elements, transformed into contractual services such as pensions, transferred to central responsibility. The process of transfer was not completed until the establishment of the National Assistance Board in 1948; up to 1939 public assistance was more responsible for the difficulties of local finance than any other single cause, at least on the expenditure side.

Small exchequer grants in aid of 'onerous' local services had been given before the mid-century; and shortly before the beginning of our period a wider system of assistance had been arranged, but in a manner which was expressly designed to interfere as little as possible with local financial autonomy. The revenue from certain central taxes was simply 'assigned' for local use, for the most part as a general aid, but a modicum was specifically earmarked for particular purposes. By this means additional practically independent revenue was made available to local authorities,[1] in 1885 amounting to £4·6 mn. and gradually rising to £11·3 mn. in 1895 and £16 mn. in 1900. This unallocated grant, however, gradually declined in relation to other local sources, including specific grants (see Table 11 below), partly through the reluctance of the Treasury to resign control over developing tax sources, partly because of the gradual discovery by the central departments, now arising in Whitehall, that the financial control of local authorities through specific grants was more effective, more flexible, and more economical to the Treasury than any feasible method of direct control.[2] In the development of a balanced and purposive grant system the Board of Education was throughout the pioneer department.

[1] In the U.K. as a whole.
[2] See D. N. Chester: *Central and Local Government.*

The exchequer grant thus became an essential element in local finance from early in the present century: that it is there for definite purposes must always be borne in mind when contemplating the otherwise melancholy story of the decline of the local rate, which from an average of about 30 per cent. of total tax revenue at the beginning of the present century fell to about 17 per cent. in the inter-war period and since 1945 has not exceeded between 7 per cent. and 8 per cent. This relative collapse of the local rate has, however, a deeper significance than the growth of the desire to control on the part of the central government. It reflects real weaknesses in the rate as a tax, which have developed on the one hand as a result of the process of de-rating of certain classes of hereditaments (fundamentally due to the pressure of rates upon them), and on the other hand to the erosion of the basis of valuation for rating through rent control. We shall have to return to this point at a later stage. In fact the expansion of exchequer grants has been more than proportional to the fall in rates since, owing to policy that was social and economic rather than fiscal, the net surpluses on local trading services declined practically to zero after the turn of the century.

If we confine our attention to England and Wales, which in any case is by far the largest part of the matter, we can without difficulty follow the development of local activities from the end of the first world war, while official estimates enable us to carry the story back to 1913. Table 9 shows the distribution of 'rate fund' (or current expenditure) between different services. The actual financing of the services was partly by rates, partly by minor local sources such as fees, fines, and licences, and partly by exchequer grants; the extent of these last we shall examine presently (see Table 11). The greater part of the story has already emerged in Chapter II since the local authorities are principle agents for the implementation of social

TABLE 9

Distribution of Rate Fund Expenditure in Selected Years, England and Wales [1]

(Percentages)

	1913	1923	1929	1933	1938	1947	1950
Education . .	32	24	26	26	25	30	41
Health . .	17	13	15	17	19	19	16
Housing, etc. .	neg.	5	11	13	11	8	14
Highways . .	17	14	16	16	12	8	10
Police . .	8	6	6	6	6	6	8
Poor Relief .	12	11	18	18	9	6	neg.
Other . .	14	27	8	4	18	23	11
	100	100	100	100	100	100	100
£mn. .	101·8	292·5	312·3	318·3	387·6	679·3	649·8

policy; but some aspects require special notice from the local point of view:

(1) The special importance of Education among the social services is apparent from the first; hardly less noticeable is its relative stagnation in the inter-war years and revived importance in the implementation of the Butler Act.

(2) The Health services cover two quite different functions: (*a*) the provision of communal works and

[1] Excluding trading services and corporation estates.

services such as sewerage, street cleansing, parks, and baths, and (*b*) individual services such as hospitals; but it is only within the last few years that it has been possible to distinguish between these in the statistics. In 1947, before the establishment of the national health service, expenditure was about equal on the two branches, but by 1950 individual services had shrunk to about one-half of communal. When local Health centres (as envisaged in the National Health Act) are developed, individual services will once more expand, but hardly as much as in the 1920s when they were an important cause of the change over from specific to block grants, or in the 1930s when many local authorities were busy adapting the newly acquired Poor Law hospitals for general use.

(3) The rise of local authority Housing in the 1920s and its culmination in the building boom of the early '30s emerges clearly; but it is notable that at no period has it been so important among local activities as in 1950; since then it has expanded further.

(4) The importance given to highway expenditure in the 1920s, which continued as long as the life of the independent Road Fund, is matched (as we have already seen in connection with the measurement of capital formation) by its utter neglect since 1945.

(5) The 'other' services, which have fluctuated greatly, have also changed their composition over the period. Development now is largely accounted for by the new services in connection with the care of children and the elderly; these two together account for about 4 per cent. out of the 11 per cent. in 1950.

(6) The most striking change of all, however, is on the side of poor relief. In 1929–33 local authorities were spending £34 mn. on this service alone; in 1929

this was about one-third more than they were receiving in non-specific grants. The relief on this head which has been afforded to them since 1948 enables them to concentrate much more effectively on constructive services.

In order to complete the picture of local activities we need to glance at expenditure on capital account, since most of the services call for the provision of fairly extensive equipment; indeed, capital expenditure serves to underline the changes that have taken place on current account, especially since 1945. The relative importance of the different services is shown in Table 10. Most striking of all is the concentration on housing, leading in 1947 to a relative neglect of almost every other type of capital formation. By 1950, however, other forms of capital investment had revived to some extent, education rising from £8 mn. to £44 mn.[1] between the two years, and health service investment from £7 mn. to £16 mn. These changes were accompanied by a heavy fall in investment in trading services —from £51·5 mn. to £35·5 mn. between the two years, through the loss of the principle trading services to the national Corporations.

The general picture that emerges is very clearly that the scope of local activities has been substantially narrowed over the period, especially by the loss of public assistance, important health services, and trading. The first is on the whole not to be regretted, for there is no clear indication that the service is not as well conducted under central control. The loss of trading services, however, removes one of the most

---

[1] As we have seen (p. 37, above) the Select Committee on the Estimates judged the rate of school building in 1953 o be still far from adequate.

attractive aspects of local councillors' work, and is to be much regretted from the local point of view. As things have now developed it is hardly too much to

TABLE 10

Distribution of Local Expenditure on Capital Account,[1]
England and Wales (Percentages)
(Selected Years)

	1913	1923	1929	1933	1938	1947	1950
Education . .	14	1	5	4	9	2	11
Health . .	16	15	7	10	11	2	4
Housing . .	3	22	39	38	36	70	62
Highways . .	15	16	14	9	9	1	1
Other non-trading . .	13	11	10	6	13	9	13
Total non-trading .	61	65	75	67	78	84	91
Trading . .	39	35	25	33	22	16	9
Grand Total	100	100	100	100	100	100	100
£mn. .	21·1	50·0	108·9	89·3	150·8	303·5	383·8

say that local authorities are mainly becoming the government's agents for the administration of education and the building of houses. This in itself, apart from the loss of the trading services, implies some loss of autonomy since these have always been the services most closely controlled by Whitehall. Before we come

[1] As represented by expenditure out of loan; a closer approximation is not possible over a period, but for a broad picture the two are sufficiently close.

to any conclusions on this, however, it is necessary to examine the resources side of local finance.

As we have seen, the most important factor on the resources side is the near collapse of the local rate, the only independent local tax of any importance. Before we discuss whether efforts could, or should, be made to restore the rate to its former place it will be advisable to look at the development of the exchequer grants which have indirectly (or in the case of compensation for de-rating, directly) taken the place of rate revenue. The scope and form of grants is vital for the question of local autonomy.

Table 11 shows that exchequer grants have been creeping up both absolutely and as a percentage of rate fund expenditure, since the beginning of the century; the slight dip in their relative importance in 1938 was due to the fall in the Housing subsidy, a fall which, as it happens, made only a moderate difference to the activity of local authorities. Much more important than this momentary fall are the three sudden upward steps: from 9 per cent. to 21 per cent. between 1900 and 1905, from 26 per cent. to 36 per cent. between 1923 and 1929 and from 41 per cent. to 46 per cent. between 1947 and 1950. All are the result of important modifications of the grant system, an important purpose of which was in every case the relief of the rates.

As appears from the table, exchequer grants have all along been of two types: specific to particular services, and non-specific, hence available in general support of rate fund expenditure; the changes in the relative importance of these two types of grant have a considerable significance, for their characteristics differ markedly. The specific grant is, generally speaking, the more promotional; the fact that special assistance is available inevitably stimulates local authorities to establish or enlarge a service. On the other hand

TABLE 11

Exchequer Grants on Current Account
Local Authorities in England and Wales
(Selected Years)

	1900	1913	1923	1929	1933	1938	1947	1950
Total Grants £mn. .	12·2	22·5	78·4	113·4	125·2	146·7	280·6	304·2
Percentages for the various services:								
Specific Grants								
Education . .	60	61	48	37	30	31	41	43
Health . . .	..	5[1]	5	5	1	1	3	5
Housing . .	..	..	9	10	10	10	8	9
Highways . .	..	2	13	16	9	9	4	4
Police and Justice .	..	12	11	9	8	8	7	8
Other Specific .	..	8	8	5	4	8[3]	15[3]	15
Non-specific Grants[2] .	40	12	6	18	38	33	22	16[4]
	100	100	100	100	100	100	100	100
Total Grants as a Percentage of Rate Fund Expenditure .	9[5]	23	26	36	39	38	41	46

specific grants tend to call for more detailed supervision; the grant is usually awarded on some particular definition of expenditure (thus the Education grant defines 'recognizable' expenditure), and it is necessary

[1] Including poor relief (pauper lunatics).
[2] Including compensation for de-rating.
[3] Including grant for special expenses arising out of the war.
[4] £49·2 mn., of which the Equalization Grant = £46·9 mn.
[5] By 1905 this had become 21 per cent.

Some grants on Capital Account are unavoidably included.

for the central administration to check that the conditions have been complied with. Thirdly the specific grant is not usually well adapted to applying differential aid to those areas whose resources are small and whose needs are great (circumstances, from the nature of the services, normally occurring together). The actual effect of any particular grant formula may, however, differ importantly according to such factors as the interest of local authorities in the service (where normally 50 per cent. would be sufficient bait it was found necessary to offer 75 per cent. for treatment of venereal disease, and nothing less than 100 per cent. would stimulate the development of air raid precautions in advance of need).

Generally speaking, in times of relative financial ease also local authorities are more likely to be drawn by a specific grant than in times of stringency. Hence it would be wrong to attempt to draw any precise conclusions concerning the effectiveness of grants by comparing Tables 9 and 10; in a general sense, however, the way in which expenditure does 'follow the grant' is quite evident.

The expansion of exchequer grants should not necessarily be considered an adverse factor in local finance; on the contrary grants may be reckoned a desirable feature in local or, for that matter, state finance in a federation, for three quite separate reasons: as a general support of local resources, for the promotion of particular services, and to secure a greater degree of equality (in some sense) between areas. Quite generally when the duties of a 'lower layer' government come to exceed the resources under its control the most convenient way of restoring equilibrium may be a grant. This may be so either because the higher government is unwilling to relinquish control over any of its taxes, perhaps because it has its eye fixed on future needs, perhaps, more respectably, because the taxes which might be made available to lower governments tend to be regressive and their expansion would disturb the progression of the tax structure in general; or perhaps merely because the lower government is technically unable to administer adequately any but a very narrow range of taxes.

In Britain the first two of these reasons have been decisive. If too much weight is put on the local rate it soon runs into difficulties. Domestic rates *are* regressive—on small incomes and large families, although, as we shall see later, not so much as is generally thought to be the case. Non-domestic rates are a charge on overheads which in itself makes it undesirable that the weight should be heavy. Most important of all, as rates rise the difference between rate levels in different areas tends to become unacceptably large, and hence to become cumulative, as those who can afford to leave the heavily rated area. An important result of British exchequer grants has been to reduce the regression of the tax structure both between incomes and between areas. Grants of this nature, intended as a subsidy to local resources, should clearly be as general as possible in order that, from the local point of view, they may be as close a substitute as possible for the additional tax source which might otherwise have been made available.

Promotion of particular services is especially called for when new services are being inaugurated; in a federation where the national government has no power to enforce they may well be the only method of bringing the services into existence. Even in a unitary country the promotional grant has been found extremely useful for stimulating interest among the more conservative authorities, who are by no means necessarily the poorest. For this purpose experience has shown that the most effective type of grant is the percentage on approved expenditure on the service, or, as in housing, where the service admits of a definition of a unit, the simple grant per unit provided. The great weakness of the promotional grant, however, is its dis-equalizing tendency; only the richer authorities can afford to take full advantage of it. This was well illustrated in the 1930s by the failure of the Welsh counties, who needed it most, to take advantage of the grant for tubercular treatment. A heavy use of percentage grants will thus inevitably lead to uneven standards of service between areas.

In recent years prime interest (though by no means pride of place) in Britain has been devoted to experimentation with equalizing grants. This is partly to be accounted for by the demonstration of the increasing tendency for rate levels to diverge, a divergence which was already giving rise to concern before the first world war. In part it is merely another manifestation of the increasing sensitiveness to inequality. The first attempt at equalization formed part of the supplementary education grant of 1917. This contained an adjustment to a combined percentage and unit grant, to allow for low rate yield. The same general form appears in the education grant today, but it is notable that the percentage element has increased relatively to the others.

The first element of equalization in a general grant was that of the 'Block' grant which in 1929 took the place of a number of specific grants, and as appears from Table 11, notably increased the proportion of non-specific grants in the structure. Only a minor part of the Block grant, however, was given on a differential basis; the major part, constituted compensation for the 75 per cent. de-rating of factories ('industrial hereditaments') and the final demise of rates on agricultural land, which were part of the same settlement. This section of the grant was given strictly in accordance with rate losses, so that the equalizing force of the whole was inevitably weak.

The equalizing section of the Block grant was based on a formula which had two distinct merits: (1) it made a genuine attempt to use objective measures of resources and needs as base for the grant, and (2) the amount of grant was determined in advance, both in respect of the total and of its distribution between authorities; it therefore caused no disturbance to either local or national budgeting.

On the other hand the objective measures chosen: on the resources side an allowance for low rateable value per head and on the needs side three factors assumed to give rise to special costs (proportion of children under five to total population, percentage of unemployed, and, in rural areas low population per mile of road), did not turn out in practice to give accurate measures of need. It was notable that the poorest areas did not qualify for especially high grants, while as time went on an increasing number of wealthy areas qualified for substantial aid. Yet the inefficiency—or rather insufficiency—of the Block grant should not be exaggerated. The conspicuous shortcomings of the formula could easily have been remedied; in fact a substantial improvement in it was effected after 1937 by increasing the weighting for high unemployment.

Greater flexibility could have been introduced by reducing the period for which the grant was fixed, say from five years to three, or by arranging for variations in amount of grant from year to year within the period. The two main reasons for the relative failure of the Block grant were first, its small coverage and secondly, the fact that public assistance remained a local responsibility. With the onset of the depression the strain on rates in certain areas became nearly as great as it had been before attempted equalization.

In spite of its real merits, however, the Block grant of 1929 was not considered a success; the next experiment in differential aid, the 'Equalization' grant of 1948, set out specifically to remedy its defects. The 1948 grant is only awarded to sub-average authorities; thus no effort is wasted on relatively wealthy authorities. Secondly, the amount of grant is determined, both in total and as to its distribution between areas, *ex post*, so that it is completely flexible from year to year. On the resources side more importance is given to rateable value per head (slightly modified by a weighting for children under fifteen and by a sparsity factor, similar in kind but differing significantly in detail, to the corresponding factor in the 1929 formula). On the needs side 'needs' are simply measured for each authority by its actual expenditure as determined by rate poundage.

The result is a grant which is much more congenial from the local point of view than the 1929 formula, so far at least as the grant-receiving authorities are concerned (seven counties and twenty-eight county boroughs failed to qualify for any grant in 1950, including several that are by no means clearly wealthy). The Equalization grant in fact amounts to a percentage grant in aid of all rate fund services, the amount of the percentage being determined on the one hand by the extent to which rateable value per head falls below the national average, and on the other by the rate poundage of the area. If the limited degree of weighting still retained in the formula were transferred to specific grants for the services where these particular causes of extra cost were relevant (for instance the weighting for children to the education grant) the Equalization grant would achieve complete equalization in the sense that (assuming rateable value per head is an adequate indicator of relative resources) equal *per capita* expenditure would lead to exactly equal rate poundages. These very merits from the local point of view, however, make the Equalization grant less commendable from the point of view of the national budget where it constitutes a type of 'open-ended' expenditure, similar in kind, although only one-tenth in amount, to that due to the national health service.

If equalization (or rather proportionality) of rate poundages is the desired aim of a differential grant, then the 1948 grant is in measurable distance of complete success; but, as first established at least, it suffers from two serious shortcomings. Rateable value per head cannot be accepted as a reliable indicator of relative resources until uniformity of valuation practice has been secured throughout the country; this is a point to which we shall have to return later. Secondly, and much more important, to award a grant exactly proportional to what each local authority chooses to spend may turn out to be inconveniently promotional. Moreover, in respect of the poorer authorities, the percentage aid implied in the grant is very high indeed. Among the counties (in 1949–50) one was receiving a grant of 66·9 per cent. of 'net relevant expenditure' (in the language of Whitehall), while four others received over 55 per cent.; among the county boroughs one received 50 per cent. and three others over 35 per cent.

Against these criticisms of the Equalization grant two defences can be advanced: (1) an equalization grant which does not equalize financial opportunities can never be satisfactory. In fact there are substantial safeguards against undue extravagance in the form of direct controls, not to mention the sanction that additional outlay will always to some extent raise the rates. In fact substantial differences in standards of general amenity services continue to exist between poor and rich areas. (2) The national government now very largely insists on national standards of service so that it may be held to be under an implicit obligation to see that the means of achieving them are generally available. In both these contentions there is considerable truth, and if the promotional element in the Equalization grant proves embarrassing it would be simple to base the measurement of needs, not on the individual rate poundage of an authority, but on some sort of average; the size of its grant would thus be taken out of the direct control grant receiving authority.

In this connection it should, however, be noted that, quite apart from the transition from the 1929 formula to the Equalization grant, the grant structure is becoming more promotional. In 1950 the three large grants for education, for police, and for highways were all basically percentage; in respect of the first, as we have already seen, the percentage element had recently been increased; the highway grants seem also to be more purely percentage and less differential than formerly. A number of the smaller specific grants, such as for fire services, are also on a percentage basis; altogether about 80 per cent. of the grant structure would seem now to be primarily on a promotional base. It is of course as much for purposes of control as of promotion that this policy has been followed.

The 1929 grant, as we have seen, wasted its equalizing efforts by giving substantial grants to wealthy areas; the Equalization grant does not make this mistake, but is in danger of going to the other extreme; by limiting its attention to sub-average authorities it leaves uncompensated differences of substantial amount. This raises the question: what do we mean by equalization? If it is equalization of rate poundages that is desired this could be achieved by much more direct methods; the same is true of the achievement of *equal* standards of service. In either case, however, the achievement of the aim would almost certainly destroy the last remnants of local autonomy.

Probably the first idea behind the differential grant was that of achieving tolerable standards of service in all areas, in an American phrase 'underwriting minimum service standards'. In Britain this aim is now regarded as too modest, and in fact substantial equality of standards in all the basic services has already been attained. Once public assistance was taken off the rates the main obstacle to this was removed. The question is how far further degrees of equalization are compatible with a continuance of a spirit of freedom of choice in local government.

It is obvious that a great deal of the traditional freedom and initiative of British local government has been lost, and with it has gone also much of the more limited freedom which existed between the wars. A great deal of this is inevitable because its continuance would not have been compatible either with the greater equalization of service standards which is now demanded, or with an integrated socio-economic policy at the national level. In other respects which are not germane to these ends, however, local authorities are now less free than they used to be. As we have seen, the narrowing of the scope of their activities has implied the loss of services in which they were especially free and the retention of those in which they are especially controlled. On the capital side also the free access to the stock exchange which was a real privilege for the larger authorities at least in the 1920s has been lost, first through the compulsory borrowing from the Public Works Loans Fund, and, when in 1952 this restriction was withdrawn, through the continuance of financial control by the Capital Issues Committee and direct control over materials by various Ministries. Finally, as we saw at an earlier stage,[1] the change in the scope of local activities has been accompanied by a greater concentration of the control of local services under the larger authorities, the counties and county boroughs; it is not by any means certain that it is in these that the lamp of local initiative burns most brightly.

Some of the changes have indeed been in the interest of the local authorities themselves; the necessity to spend a large part of rate revenue on public assistance was more destructive of local initiative than the removal of dis-equalizing services. In general however it cannot reasonably be contended that the loss of freedom is of no account. If there is to be any virtue or any truth in local government two things are necessary: first that a range of activities should continue to be available

[1] Chapter I.

which will attract and hold the interest of the citizens and so secure that the best types are elected to local councils; secondly that the zeal and interest of both councillors and administrators are not lost in a maze of frustration and delay in Whitehall. In spite of all that has happened there are a few reasons for hoping that the situation is not yet too desperate, although it is unquestionably dangerous.

In the first place, and in spite of the high proportion of grants to rates in some areas, local freedom of budgeting—the ability of local councils to determine the total of their expenditure and to lay out the funds at their disposal between different services according to local desires—is still considerably more than formal. The situation in Britain is very different from that, for instance, in many American cities where state charters put an absolute ceiling on the level of the local property tax (the opposite number to the rate), so that the proper development of even basic municipal services is seriously hindered. Secondly, although a high proportion of grants inevitably implies a wider degree of control by Whitehall than formerly, with the general rise in administrative standards it becomes increasingly possible for control to be concentrated at certain key points only (this has been agreed both by central and local administrators).[1] In this way much of the delay and frustration experienced both by local councillors and their officers in the inter-war years should be avoided.

Finally, the narrowed scope of local government has still left a considerable range of matters of great local interest and importance. This is true of education, of the

[1] See Report of the Local Government Manpower Committee, 1951.

new services now being worked out for health centres and for the care of children and the aged, and above all it is true of housing. Housing, which as we have seen, is now more important in local government than it has ever been, has two particular advantages from the present point of view: it is concerned not only with immediate problems of management and social betterment, but also with the future. It includes interests that are æsthetic and educational as well as those that are social and economic. Secondly, housing is not a monopoly of the larger authorities; indeed it is not a county matter at all; even the smallest rural district has its part to play. Thus housing may well be capable of supplying and preserving just that strictly local element of interest which we have argued to be necessary for the survival of live local government.

Nevertheless, while there is still hope for the future of British local government as an independent entity in the economy, the extreme tenuousness of the strand of independent tax powers is an ever-present danger. We must therefore finally turn to examine the weaknesses of the local rate and the prospects of its rehabilitation, or in the event of that proving impossible, partial supersession by more promising sources of local finance.

We argued in the last chapter that the local rate was in principle a good tax, especially for local purposes. The occupation of house room is so widely distributed in consumption that a very large revenue can be raised at quite low rates of tax. Nor is the formal incidence of the rate violently regressive; in a number of income ranges it is probable that expenditure on house room broadly keeps pace with rising incomes so that the tax is proportional rather than regressive. In any case the important factor from the social point of view is not so much the progression or regression of an individual tax (unless it is obviously anti-social, which the rate clearly is not) as the combined progression of the entire tax structure. In Britain this is entirely within the control of the national government; in fact, the relative expansion of exchequer grants, financed from a progressively based tax pool, has materially reduced the regressive element in local finance.

From the specifically local point of view the rate has further advantages. The base, the land and buildings of the area, is unequivocally localized; it cannot be disputed by any other authority, as could a local income tax. Moreover, since real estate values and rents change only slowly, the rate base has just that steadiness which is so necessary for local governments with their many fixed obligations and limited resources. Further, and most important of all, the rate is admirably fitted to be the balancing factor in local budgets; once the value of the area has been ascertained it is a matter of simple arithmetic to determine what poundage must be levied to pay for each service; the relation between tax and service is thus obvious to ratepayers. Viewed in this light the local rate has been of incalculable advantage in building up a spirit of responsibility among local taxpayers. That it can still serve this purpose has recently been demonstrated in some West African territories, where the local populations were, previous to the introduction of a rate-type of local tax, unwilling to find the finance for services that they vociferously demanded.

Yet in spite of its many virtues the enemies of the local rate have ever been more vocal than its friends; and this is no less true now that is has shrunk so considerably in relation to other taxes than when it was the principle source of revenue. This hostility is probably partly due to a misapprehension of the rate in relation to ability to pay. It is thought on the one hand that its regression is greater than the available statistics suggest, and on the other that a local tax, like a central tax, should be directly related to 'ability to pay', regardless of the regression of many important central taxes.

More fundamentally, hostility to the rate is probably caused by the fact that although it is in principle an outlay tax, based on the rent of premises occupied and not on the economic position of the occupier, it is yet an intensely personal tax. This is the more true because the local councillors who fix the poundage are usually well known in the district and can be criticized personally. Ratepayers are thus abnormally sensitive, especially in the county boroughs where the same authority is responsible for all services; in a county district the remote County Council is known to be responsible for the greater part of the poundage, so that the local councillors can disclaim any power in the matter.

It is unfortunate in this respect that rate liability is commonly thought of in terms of the poundage only (and the different significance of a rate from an income tax poundage is perhaps not always fully realized). True rate liability depends of course on valuation, based on rent, multiplied by the local poundage; but valuation is obscure and unknown, while differences between poundages are obvious to all; yet unless related to valuations they are meaningless. For instance between 1913 and 1920 average rate poundages roughly doubled but valuations hardly rose, so that in terms of constant prices (or of war-inflated incomes) rate liability actually fell.

Nevertheless, in the inter-war years, especially in the late '20s before the introduction of the Block grant, the real burden of rates presented a real problem, the most important aspect of which was the divergence between the level in different areas. In this public assistance was all along the villain of the piece. In 1927 six authorities and in 1928 five authorities were spending on poor relief alone between 65s. and 125s. per head, corresponding to poundages of from 9s. to 12s., while the more fortunate authorities were spending less than 5s. per head, corresponding to a poundage of less than 6d. After the 1929 reforms, which included a wider spreading of liability for poor rates as the small areas of the Guardians were abolished, rates indeed were still high; but in 1932, the worst year of the depression, the highest *per capita* expenditure for poor relief did not exceed 40s. On the average, total rate poundages fell from 12s. 10½d. in 1928 to 10s. 10d. in 1933. The transfer to a national authority of responsibility for the able-bodied poor in 1934, combined with the operation of the Block grant kept the situation in hand; but towards the end of the '30s both the average level of rates and their dispersion were again increasing. In 1938–9 among the county boroughs poundages ranged from 27s. 6d. to just over 7s., but only three areas had a poundage exceeding 20s. The difficulties of the war again caused some deterioration in the position (but the effect of the fall in the value of money in increasing both absolute height and absolute differences must be taken into account). In 1947–8 the highest county borough was using a poundage of 39s. 11d. and the lowest 10s. 9d., with an average of 19s. 6d. The following year, in spite of a rising level of local expenditure, the operation of the Equalization grant had reduced the average poundage to 18s. 11d., the lowest to 12s. 1d. and the highest to 25s. 8d. The operation of the Equalization grant will effectively prevent a return to the inter-war situation at any time in the future.

Nevertheless, even at the 1938 levels the local rate was not a heavy tax, even in the highest-rated areas. The formal incidence on the lower income groups is shown below for Wales, the area in the country with the highest rates poundages, and for the southern areas where they were especially low. All other areas lay between these limits, except London which has exceptionally high rates, but since it is not poor is presumably satisfied that the services are desirable.

Average (annual) Family Expenditure	Rates (1938–9) as a Percentage of Average Family Expenditure	
£	Wales	South England
150	5·3	3·5
200	4·3	3·0
250	3·6	2·8
300	3·1	2·6

Although rate poundages were exceptionally high in Wales, the total cost of house services (rents plus rates) were lower than in the south; for the same income range of families gross rents in Wales averaged 24s. 1d. a week and in the south of England 27s.; but no doubt the houses in the south were better worth while.

If we allow for the change in the value of money since 1938 and reflect that the family who spent £150 in 1938 would have at its command at least £300 in

1950 (in Wales the increase would be even greater owing to the improved employment position), the highest rate incidence at 1938 poundages could not have exceeded 3·1 per cent. of income in 1950; in fact this is probably an over-estimate since it is just the highest-rated areas of 1938 which have benefited most by the transfer of poor relief, and by the operation of the Equalization grant.

In spite of a probable fall in the propensity to submit to rates as other taxes (especially income tax) rise, it can hardly be doubted that rates could now without hardship be restored at least to their 1938 position in relation both to personal incomes and to the national income. By this means it would probably be possible to provide something like an extra £100 mn. of *independent* revenue for local authorities, *ceteris paribus*. Unfortunately, however, a serious difficulty has arisen in the assessment of the rate which, while it need not make the restoration of the rate position impossible, does certainly complicate it. The difficulty is concerned with the valuation basis; it thus concerns the Equalization grant (with its dependence on rateable value per head as a measurement of relative needs) as much as it does the well-being of the rate; a solution of the problem is thus of first urgency for local finance.

The basis of valuation on which the rate rests is the free market rent of the 'hereditament'. It was always common knowledge, however, that (except north of the Tweed where the use of the actual rent was obligatory) rateable value often differed markedly from what the free market rent would have been for a new lease. Before 1925 there was no general obligation outside London to keep valuations up to date by regular revaluations of the entire property of the district.

Consequently relative levels of assessment came to differ markedly according as a recent valuation had, or had not, been made. So long as no grants were based on relative rateable values this was a matter of indifference between areas, but not of course between property of different ages within areas. From 1917, however, as we have seen, the important Education grant came to be based partly on rateable values, and from that time the importance for the grant system of uniform valuation practice all over the country has steadily increased. When the 1929 formula was drawn up it was recognized that valuation practice was far from uniform; consequently no great weight was put on relative rateable values. When the Equalization grant was introduced it was confidently anticipated that a uniform system of valuation would be evolved and applied within a very short period. The failure of this expectation to be realized is a weakness—although probably not so serious a weakness as is sometimes considered—in the whole system.

Before 1914 the differences in the level of assessment seem to have been random and accidental, so that they could probably have been ironed out by regular revaluations. With the impact of rent control in the first war, however, for the first time they began to be systematic as between different types of property, and as a consequence between different areas according to the importance in them of one type of property or another. In particular the smaller pre-1914 houses tended (against the view of the courts) to be valued nearer to their controlled rents than to what their free market rents would have been in terms of post-war prices. Small new houses in turn tended to be valued with the older small houses, rather than by their own rents. In this way by 1938 a substantial underrating of small houses had become general over the country, and was especially important in the home counties where there had been much new building of this type. In justice there was a clear case either for formalizing, and hence controlling, this accidental 'derating', or for bringing it to an end. The government, however, became frightened of the possible effects on the family budgets of the occupiers of the undervalued houses (who were often also the owners and hence particularly vulnerable) of applying full valuation to this type of property; and no very obvious method of circumscribing the effects presented itself. Hence the whole problem was postponed for further consideration, only to be complicated still further within a year by the impact of the total rent control of the second world war.

The problem of restoring equilibrium to the valuation system, so that uniform methods are applied all over the country, has so far defeated the ingenuity of administrators. A first step was taken when in 1948 the business of valuation was centralized; however much local authorities may regret this change it was clearly desirable from the point of view of straightening out inter-local differences of practice. The Valuation for Rating Act of 1953 attempts a second step by imposing a single valuation basis for domestic rates: actual or imputed rents at June 1939. Since the de-rating of industry and agriculture the rate has become predominantly a tax on domestic and business premises, including shops; but this is not necessarily right or desirable. The arguments which led to de-rating in 1929 to a large extent no longer hold, and it should seriously be considered whether a measure (not

K

necessarily 100 per cent.) of re-rating should not now be resorted to; this would at one stroke lighten the burden on domestic rates (thus easing the problem of eliminating anomalies), widen the basis of local taxation and at the same time give help to industrial towns which under the Equalization grant have lost their compensation for de-rating.

Its best friends however cannot deny that rent control has seriously, and perhaps permanently, undermined the basis of the rate. It is very desirable therefore that a diligent search should be made for other independent sources of local revenue. Unfortunately in Britain with the present pressure on the revenue, prospects are not encouraging. It is hardly conceivable that the Treasury could be persuaded to part with any source of revenue more important than the Entertainments tax, and even of this there is no immediate hope. While such a transfer would not solve the problem of independent local finance the £50 mn. which could easily be raised from it would be most welcome, especially as it would accrue mainly in urban areas which incur considerable costs in respect of their non-resident day populations.

Another source of local revenue which has frequently been advocated is a local income tax, or a percentage added to the national tax. Apart from the difficulties of defining the location of income, this would be considerably more dis-equalizing between areas than the rate, even if it were not progressive; there is also the problem of compatibility with high national taxes. The most practicable form of local income tax for this country would seem to be a proportional tax levied without reliefs on all income arising within the area, which would be allowed as a cost for national income tax.

This would embody many of the advantages of rates while yet being less regressive in incidence.

Another suggestion which has been put forward is for a rate on site values, in addition to the rate on the combined hereditament of site and building. In developing countries a tax of this nature has been found to be a useful stimulus to building, in contrast to a tax of the nature of the British rate, which is in the long run a tax on building (although this can largely be overcome by housing subsidies). In a stationary economy the attractions of a site value rate are much less obvious, while the more built-up the valuation areas are the more difficult does the problem of valuation become. Valuation, as we have seen, is sufficiently complicated when the hereditament as a whole is to be valued; for the site alone of a built-up area it appears to be almost unsurmountable. It is unlikely therefore that a site value rate would go far to solve our problems in Britain today.

Here we must leave the problem; but it must be emphasized that until some means is discovered of restoring the independence of local finance at least to the inter-war position, we must continue to regard local autonomy, with all that it implies for the future of a firmly founded democracy, as being still on the danger list.

Chapter V

BUDGET BALANCE AND
NATIONAL BALANCE

WE must now turn back to the question left open in Chapter III: the significance of the balance of revenue and expenditure and the role of the Budget in the economy. When we are concerned with the global effect of public finance on the level of incomes and economic stability in an economy, it has become customary to talk of *fiscal policy*. Although this term is not etymologically correct (since it should refer only to the tax side) it is a convenient short cut and we may reasonably allow ourselves to use it. Fiscal policy in the sense of a purposeful marshalling of the armoury of public finance in order to influence the level of incomes cannot be said to have been recognized as an art before the middle or late 1930s. Up to that time considerations of public finance ran in terms only of the effects of individual taxes and outlays, on particular aspects of economic life, without regard to the total effect.

It should not therefore hastily be concluded that policy related to the whole economy did not receive due attention in Victorian England or that any decisively new factor entered into consideration in the 1930s, nor, more especially, that this new outlook had any inherent party political flavour. Such an attitude appears to be common in the U.S.A. and is not unreasonable as applied to that country. There was no such thing there as budgetary policy in the modern sense until the establishment of the Bureau of the

Budget in 1921, while then, and until much later, the Ways and Means and Finance Committees of Congress, whose business it was to review the tax structure, thought of themselves as mainly concerned to construct an effectively protective tariff.

In England the duty of public authorities to adjust their policy so as to promote stability in the economy had been expounded in the middle 1820s by Horsley Palmer, the Governor of the Bank of England, and again, with outstanding clarity, by Walter Bagehot in the 1870s; but it was always assumed that the chosen vessel would be the Bank of England's credit control, and not fiscal policy. Although the Bank of England was not legally nationalized until 1946 it was formally recognized as a public authority, and from the time of the Bank Act of 1844 this position was made additionally clear by the need to resort to Treasury permission before undertaking the kind of expansion that might be required in depression.

In spite of this continuity in the recognition of the responsibility of public authorities for stability policy, the contrast between Victorian practice and recent policy is profound. Credit control has been reduced to an instrument of secondary importance compared to fiscal policy, and between 1940 and 1951 was almost entirely in abeyance in the normal sense.[1] In fiscal policy the modern world has discovered an instrument of control of first-rate importance. Nevertheless in England it is the means rather than the end which is new; in promoting stability fiscal policy should be considered as an addition to rather than as a substitute for credit policy.

That no one should have conceived of fiscal policy

[1] See Chapter VI.

in the modern sense in Victorian times is due to a number of causes. The most obvious is the small size of the public sector, and hence the ineffectiveness of policy on the level of incomes. As we have seen, in the 1870s and for most of the 1880s, the public sector did not exceed 10 per cent. to 11 per cent. of the economy; until the development of local trading services public investment did not exist outside the Post Office, which brought in a net revenue of about £2 mn. There could hardly be a greater contrast from the public sector of today absorbing about 40 per cent. of the national income and undertaking over 50 per cent. of gross capital formation. If the theory on which modern fiscal policy is based had not been developed, actually somewhat in advance of the final upsurge of the public sector which led to these figures, it would have been necessary in any case to have evolved some method of putting this vast power on a leash, lest it should work havoc in the economy. In fact the two processes of the expansion of the public sector and the development of the theory of fiscal policy have proceeded simultaneously and have interacted upon each other.

Although they had no fiscal policy in the modern sense, the Victorians had a very definite tax-and-budget policy which paved the way for fiscal policy. The basic aim on the tax side was to keep taxes as low as possible in order to minimize the disturbance to business. Outlay taxes in particular were disliked because of their effect on prices; the movement towards free trade (the reduction of customs duties) was in its early stages at least equally a movement away from excise taxes. On the other hand, income tax was regarded as a temporary affliction to be reserved primarily for emergencies, at least as late as the middle 1870s. The first corollary drawn from this attitude was that expenditure must at all costs be kept down in order to avoid levying the taxes.

Until the demand for social expenditure gained real momentum (which, as we have seen, can hardly be dated before the late 1880s) strain on the revenue was almost wholly due to defence needs, and consequently fluctuated with the stability of the Balance of Power abroad. Later, when it became clear that a steady rise in public expenditure was unavoidable, a different corollary was implicitly drawn: that the increase in taxes, if it must come, could best be borne by income tax. In this there was little social or distributional argument; until 1909–10 income tax remained strictly proportional, although as early as 1870 the Radical leaders were demanding a 'tax free breakfast table', partly at least on distributional grounds. The aim of Victorian tax policy was thus primarily economic; an increase in income tax could be the lesser of two evils because at the low rates then anticipated it would lead to no loss of effort on the part of the taxpayer and to no distortion of prices. The fear of the effect of income tax —even of a progressive income tax—on personal savings had largely disappeared by the first decade of the present century, although Asquith paid handsome lip-service to it when introducing supertax in 1909.

On the budgetary side Victorian policy insisted that the Chancellor must always plan for a balanced budget, save in the most severe emergency. In order to ensure this he must in fact aim at an overbalance. A budget surplus was regarded as essential for two purposes in particular. In the first place (presuming that it had been obtained by an economy in expenditure or a 'natural' increase in the revenue) it would enable tax rates to be reduced; since this applied especially to taxes on outlay, a fall in the prices of consumption goods would follow; demand (assumed to be ever expanding) would be stimulated so that the final result would be both an expansion of consumers' real income and some, perhaps complete, recovery in the revenue to its old level. In circumstances in which on the one hand the population was rapidly increasing, and on the other wage-earners were still only in process of acquiring their convenient consumption habits in tobacco, tea, sugar and other easily taxable commodities, this was by no means an illusory hope.

In the second place a budget surplus was important because it would enable some reduction in the national debt to be made. In circumstances in which revenue possibilities were still only semi-developed (as they are today in an 'underdeveloped' country), and when in consequence every little war scare might lead to an increase in the debt and a rise in long-term interest rates which could not be controlled (nor its effect mitigated by gentle inflation as it could be under modern conditions), this again was not unreasonable. Up to 1874 in fact an overbalanced budget was assured in every year in which national income was rising (as it was most of the time), since revenue estimates were based on the results of the previous year which would automatically be exceeded. After that date, however, owing to a change in the practice of estimating, an overbalanced budget had to be arranged for deliberately; partly because of this, partly because the most rapidly expansionary phase of the British economy was already drawing to a close, budget surpluses became less frequent.

There was also an additional justification for the

theory of the everbalanced budget which in the mind of Gladstone in particular assumed very great importance. This was concerned with what is now generally called 'accountability control' of the public departments: securing that the sums voted by Parliament for particular purposes should not be over-spent and should be applied only to those purposes for which they had been voted. It is worth pausing over this point for a moment since from the point of view of the use of the budget as an instrument of policy the great achievement of the Victorians was the forging of a precise weapon. Although the essential steps to secure accountability control had already been taken in the 1860s, throughout the 1880s, and later the process of improving the machinery went on, both in the sense of fitting it more closely for its traditional purposes and of adapting it to the ever-expanding range of public activities.

The first step in the forging of the budget instrument was the centralization of the channels of revenue and expenditure in the Consolidated Fund. On the revenue side the major process of centralization had already been achieved before the mid-century (1846); from that time all taxes were paid directly into the central pool of the Consolidated Fund instead of passing directly to the spending departments. On the outlay side the process was more protracted and by the 1880s outlay, especially of the defence departments, was far from being fully integrated with the national system of finance; this is one explanation of the rigid economy which it was attempted to force on the Services in mid-Victorian times, even to the point at times of a dangerous parsimony. Once centralization of government intake and outlay had been achieved with fair comprehensiveness the changes in the balance of the Consolidated Fund at the Bank of England automatically revealed the state of the national financse.

The second step in creating the modern budget instrument was the enforcement of uniformity and regularity in accounting methods and in actual outlay. For this purpose Gladstone had devised two instruments: the Department of Exchequer and Audit (presided over by the Comptroller and Auditor General) and the Public Accounts Committee, a Select Committee of the House of Commons; these were created in 1861 and 1866 respectively. Regularity was thus facilitated and watched over both at the administrative and at the legislative level. Both of these institutions owed much to the influence and support of the Treasury which was steadily growing in stature as the centre of the web of financial administration, a position it has been improving and consolidating ever since.

Hand in glove, the Department of Exchequer and Audit and the 'P.A.C.' slogged away until petty irregularities had been eliminated and all departments were keeping uniform accounts on a strictly cash basis. These could within their own limitations be completely accurate, because pretending to do no more than present a record of completed transactions, no room for differences of judgment existed. It was a corollary of this system on the one hand that there should be careful accounting for any fees, fines, or other 'Appropriations in Aid' paid directly into departments (so that precise nett expenditure would be apparent), on the other that unexpended balances should be returned to the Consolidated Fund by the departments at the end of the financial year.

This dual system of control still operates, although inevitably with less precision than in the simple Victorian days; it is reinforced by a dual system of liaison officers between the central finance departments (the Treasury and the Department of Exchequer and Audit) and the spending departments. On the disbursement side the Accounting Officer (normally the Head of his Department) is personally responsible for all expenditure that takes place, and represents his department in all investigations by the Treasury, the Department of Exchequer and Audit and the P.A.C.; on the checking side officers of the Department of Exchequer and Audit work continuously on the accounts of a department, exercising a sort of running audit in advance of the formal audit carried out within the Department of Exchequer and Audit after the end of the financial year. This system both eliminates the delays which occur in many countries through the need to have a 'pre-audit' or checking of vouchers by another department before expenditure can be authorized, and also avoids the *pis aller* of 'period rationing' of expenditure, which may be said to be a sign of a want of proper contacts between the central finance department and spending departments and agencies.

Once this centralization and regularization of the public finances had been achieved—a process which should be measured in decades rather than in years—the balanced budgetary system gave a complete mirroring of the relation of revenue and expenditure, almost from week to week, certainly by the end of the financial year: on the one side of appropriation against estimate, on the other of disbursement against appropriation. The Consolidated Fund thus became a unique instrument for registering the success of control.

The machinery thus established in Gladstonian England contributed much not only to the thoroughness of accountability control but also to the forging of an effective budget instrument when it became important for economic reasons also that expenditure should take place within a particular framework of time and place. The machinery still functions, but it has been modified from the original intentions in several respects. Administrators have become more expert than they used to be so that the type of detailed check formerly exercised by the P.A.C. can now be adequately enforced at the administrative level. As the scope of government activities widened it became increasingly difficult to insist on the return of departmental balances at the end of the year, so that the perfect mirroring of the system became blurred. The change which had occurred received legislative recognition in 1921; from that time the emphasis of the reports of both the Comptroller and Auditor General and of the P.A.C. has shifted more in the direction of a broad view (including the tendering of advice on financial problems) and away from detailed examination.

In times of special strain on expenditure, as in wartime, Parliament early developed the habit of an additional safeguard in the form of an ad hoc select committee on expenditure. The most successful of this series was the Committee on Expenditure Arising out of the War which functioned in the second world war, and which became in fact the precedent for an additional piece of permanent control machinery at the legislative level: the Select Committee on the Estimates, established in 1946. Now that this Committee has been supplied with an adequate secretariat—the want of which long handicapped it and its predecessors relatively to the P.A.C.—(which effectively makes use of the staff of the Department of Exchequer and Audit), it is evident that it can play a useful part in drawing attention to waste and inefficiency in the public services of a kind that previously tended to slip through the meshes of the control machinery, because it might be too closely related to policy to be within the scope of administrative control. The Estimates Committee is especially suitable for showing up the additional costs of such things as inadequate initial planning, un-balanced development, or changes of plan after a project has been started. Often indeed this is the fault of the Cabinet or of Parliament rather than of the administration. Wastes of this nature are specially likely to arise in the Service Departments and it is significant that the Estimates Committee seems to have allocated one of its subcommittees permanently to defence expenditure.

There is however a fundamental difference between the type of control which a select committee can exercise over expenditure as it is taking place, and control over the audited accounts. The first is inevitably mainly advisory in character, as nothing must be done to weaken administrative responsibility. The P.A.C. examinations are in contrast more of the nature of a tribunal—and are deliberately given that flavour—whose findings are mandatory. The value of the work of the Estimates Committee would be enhanced if accounting methods appropriate to the different activities of departments were in use. This is a large question which we shall have to examine later.

The final Gladstonian reform which is relevant for

budgetary policy was the improvement introduced in the method of arranging and presenting the budget accounts. Under Gladstone the budget explicitly assumed the character of a comprehensive annual statement of central government expenditure and revenue for the year just ending, set against its estimates, and accompanied by estimates for the year just starting, first on the basis of existing tax rates, then with adjustments necessary to secure the desired balance. The whole plan was set out by Gladstone for the Committee of Supply (the whole House in somewhat informal guise) with the utmost clarity and with a high degree of detail. The House was, as it were, taken by the hand and invited to participate in planning (in fact their powers were fairly strictly limited by the existence of the standing order [1] which allows only the government to make suggestions calling for additional revenue). Gladstone also worked hard to improve the 'annuality' of the budget, by ensuring that the revenue and expenditure proper to the year would be collected and disbursed respectively within it.

Other Chancellors were naturally not always able to set out their Financial Statements with Gladstone's mastery; but a standard had been set and any serious weakening from it provoked immediate and scathing comment. As time went on further improvements in budgetary practice were made which substantially improved the precision of the budgetary instrument. Rigid annuality is not an unmixed blessing, as has increasingly been found as public activities extend into longer-term projects; but its basic justification, that public finance transactions should take place in the period for which they are planned, becomes more rather

[1] Now Standing Order 78.

than less important. This could in practice be combined with the consideration of a longer span of years in the budget debates.

During all this period changes in budgetary practice were not accompanied by any change in the theory of the ever-balanced budget, although as time went on the tendency to 'go soft' in depressed years and to avoid covering a temporary deficit by raising tax rates became more discernible. This policy was especially marked during the Chancellorship of Winston Churchill from 1925–29. An unequalled ingenuity was displayed in producing a balanced budget out of what was on any reasonable reckoning a deficit. Although in the employment situation of the times the instinct was sound, this of course was not the way to do things. The first time an open deficit of any substantial dimensions (not more than £40 mn. in each of two years) was allowed to develop in peacetime (and that indirectly on the insurance funds rather than on the budget) was under the Labour Government of 1929–31. The reactions to this modest deviation from orthodoxy were drastic. The Treasury retaliated by announcing that 'continued state borrowing on the present vast scale without provision for repayment by the (Unemployment) Fund will quickly call in question the stability of the British financial system'. The Chancellor, Snowden, a strict adherent to Gladstonian orthodoxy, hastened to reverse engines, and in the notorious second budget of 1931 both increased tax rates and enforced economy cuts upon public employees and pensioners. In this he was, for the time being at least, contributing to the deepening of the depression in two ways.

This demonstration more than anything else brought

into the open the loss of confidence in the theory of the ever-balanced budget which had gradually been gaining ground, not only in Britain with its problem of long unemployment inherited from the first world war and intensified by the operation of the post-war gold standard, but in many other countries also, as the depression hit first one and then another. The loss of confidence in the old ways, however, was not operating in a vacuum; already the theory of the budget as an instrument of compensatory finance was taking shape. The Keynesian analysis of depression in the form of an excess of planned saving over planned investment had already appeared in the Treatise on Money in the early days of 1931; but as yet the remedy was conceived in terms of credit policy, although the analysis of the 'multiplier' (or the serial effects on employment of a 'dose' of public expenditure in conditions of unemployed resources), appeared later in the same year. Attention was thus drawn to the possibilities of an expansion of public expenditure to fight depression, although the opportunities for such a policy were strictly limited so long as the international gold standard was adhered to.

The rationale of compensatory finance as it began to be understood in the 1930s [1] was simply that when the tide was running strongly in one direction in the economy, public authorities should throw their weight heavily in the opposite direction. Thus if private citizens and firms spent and invested less, public authorities should spend and invest more, and vice

[1] The most elaborate exposition was that of the Swedish Royal Commission on Unemployment reporting in the late '30s; as a result of this the Swedish government reformed its Budget with the express aim of facilitating an economic fiscal policy, both of stability and of development.

versa in boom conditions. In conditions of the '30s with high unemployment everywhere, there was no difficulty in discerning the direction in which public authorities should move. Nor were there any social or economic inhibitions in the way of an economically correct fiscal policy, once the abandonment of the gold standard permitted the international balance to adjust itself to the internal situation. Economically correct fiscal policy coincided with a congenially expansionary social policy. Abundant provision of all materials implied that any expansion which was technically feasible would be very unlikely to run into bottlenecks in supply, much less encounter a generally inflationary condition of shortages. In fact the difficulties of implementing compensatory finance in depression were mainly technical and institutional.

Simple depression-fighting compensatory fiscal policy, as practised in a number of countries in the late '30s (but only in Sweden with any specially devised budgetary machinery), was not capable of generalization to the opposite problem of fighting inflation. Experience of the first world war had already indicated that merely to tax more and to allow less for civilian consumption provided an insufficient defence against strong inflationary pressure. In different, but also inflationary, conditions after 1945 a simple reversal of the depression mechanism was also hardly feasible. Budget deficits and expansionary finance are popular with the man in the street; budget surpluses forced by heavy taxation require to be justified by persuading people first, that the free play of inflationary forces is more unpleasant, and secondly that the degree of disinflation planned is the minimum that will restore stability.

A mechanism for measuring the required *quantity* as

L

well as indicating the correct direction of compensatory fiscal policy was therefore called for. This was supplied by Keynes in two short works published early in the war.[1] The analysis they contained was not new; it was essentially one of a disequilibrium between effective demand and potential supply, already made public in 1935 in *The General Theory of Employment*. The quantitative and statistical basis was, however, substantially new.

In the depression analysis of the *General Theory* the argument ran that if the volume of spending on current and investment account together in an economy (including both the public and private sectors) is insufficient to pay for all the goods and services which might be produced with the available resources, there will be unemployment and a level of income lower than might have been obtained. Turning this on its head, if the amounts which the public and private sectors together attempt to spend and invest exceed the possible volume of production and imports, there will be over-full employment and inflationary pressure. The government must therefore cut down the volume of spending and investing to the point where the *national* budget will balance—in wartime by rationing, controls, and the encouragement of saving; in other circumstances it may be hoped, also to some extent by cutting down its own outlay, rather than by resort to rationing.

The novelty in the application of this analysis lay in the discovery that the point to which effective demand would have to be cut down could in principle be statistically determined, by means of estimates of the relevant economic forces determining the level

[1] *How to Pay for the War*, and 'Income and Fiscal Potential of Great Britain', in *Economic Journal*, December 1939.

of effective demand, set against the total resources available, as revealed by calculations of the national income, or gross national product.

A very similar technique of 'national housekeeping', as they called it, had actually been worked out in the Netherlands just before the war, although this was not realized in England; it was also evolved independently in Norway during the Occupation. War finance in Britain was geared to the new technique in 1941, the year of the first official estimates of the National Income; and from shortly afterwards in the U.S.A. and Canada. With the aid of rationing and the controls of labour and materials which were part of the war set-up, it proved possible to turn Britain into a planned economy almost overnight. In order to plan fiscal policy quantitatively an array of additional statistics was required; these were collected and marshalled respectively by two new government establishments: the Central Statistical Office and the Economic Section of the Cabinet Office. In all of this the hand of Keynes, by that time firmly established at the Treasury, was very evident.

The whole mechanism worked from the outset with such apparent smoothness that it was not really perceived that war conditions provided exceptionally favourable conditions for the experiment. The very existence of controls made additional statistical information immediately available, while rationing and the uncertainty of life in wartime reduced (although only temporarily) the pressure of inflation by greatly stimulating the propensity to save.

Once the new machinery of fiscal policy had been established, it appeared that it could be put to alternative uses after the war. Either it could be attempted to project into the post-war economy a type of semi-planning on the wartime model, but for the purpose of implementing a definite socio-economic policy, which was conceived in terms both of stability at a high level of activity and of development. Alternatively the new statistical apparatus could be used, less ambitiously, to quantify compensatory fiscal policy and thus obtain more precise and flexible results than had been possible in the pre-war world. The first alternative called for the formation and execution of an integrated programme in at least the major economic categories of investment, foreign trade, and government finance for the whole economy. The aim of the second would be first, to ensure that the fullest possible information concerning economic relations and tendencies was available to all who had to make economic decisions, so as to 'steer' the private sector intelligently into a policy which was economically correct. In this way the task of compensatory finance would be greatly lightened. It would then call for a careful alignment of the Budget and all other public activities to secure not merely a budget balance of the required magnitude, but also thereby a comprehensive national balance.

The first of these alternatives was attempted between 1945 and 1951 in Britain and the welfare states of Western Europe; the second was the policy followed most conspicuously in the U.S.A. and Canada. Although the two alternatives are logically distinct, in practice they merge almost imperceptibly into each other; it would perhaps be more correct to speak of a difference of emphasis rather than of a fundamental divergence of policy, at least so far as the more moderate advocates of policy are concerned. Especially in the early post-war years, however, the differences in emphasis were considerable, and not unnaturally the aims of national policies did not precisely coincide, some being geared more in the economic (developmental [1]) direction, others in the social.

The manner in which it was proposed to continue the planned economy in Britain was set out in the first of the series of Economic Surveys, which since 1947 have added to the information concerning the economic health of the nation available at the beginning of each financial year.[2] There were to be three sets of plans: (i) for individual industries, including 'targets' of output for all the most important ones; (ii) a set of 'economic budgets' including the estimates of national income and expenditure broken down in as detailed a way as possible, so as to show the 'social accounts' or money flows between one sector of the economy and the others (consumers, firms, public authorities, and so on), these accounts being arranged on an integrated system so that a debit on one account appeared as a credit on another. There was further to be a man-power budget, indicating the extent of labour 'redeployment' which would be required in order to reach the targets. Finally (iii) a third set of plans would come into play when the accounts of the nation had been drawn up and set out, and would relate to such over-riding considerations as supplies of foreign exchange, of fuel and power and of steel.

When this information had all been gathered and set out it was the duty of a central Planning Committee to reconcile the plans so as to secure compatibility,

[1] Especially for instance in the Netherlands.
[2] The most important documents previously available being the Financial Statements accompanying the Budget Speeches and (from 1941) the annual estimates of National Income and Expenditure.

and to advise on the alternative means available for obtaining a national balance. The final decisions on policy would of course be taken at the Ministerial level.

In this programme, it will be observed, development has the formal priority, balance or stability is imposed at the final level; in practice the starting point for planning seems to have been the maintenance of full employment as a datum, and both development and stability were subservient to this. In practice also it did not prove possible to implement development in the manner proposed, since consumption chronically exceeded the forecast, and this absorbed too great a volume of resources. Home private investment was at first far above the forecast, but fortunately for the balance of the economy, productivity—the output of goods and services—was also higher than anticipated, while public investment failed to reach expectations.

In general, however, a condition of substantial inflationary pressure persisted, due fundamentally to excess consumption, so that in practice heavy emphasis had to be placed on a disinflationary policy. Since a reduction in the programme of the public sector was held to be impracticable, balance must needs be obtained by running as large a budget surplus as could be managed, and, for the rest, by the continuance of a wide range of control, allocation and rationing. As the years passed the attempt to reach definite targets sank into the background, since it was obvious that they could not be obtained without much more control over labour distribution than was acceptable. The emphasis of the Economic Surveys noticeably shifted from plan for the future to record of the past, thus approximating to the American statements of 'The Nation's Economic Budget'.

There were several reasons for the failure to realize the original intentions of the semi-planned economy in Britain between 1945 and 1951; indeed we can trace them along four lines: (*i*) inconsistency of aims; (*ii*) inadequacy of statistical data, perhaps also (at least at first) insufficient realization of the limitations of essentially static statistical measurement as applied to essentially dynamic concepts such as the 'inflationary gap'; (*iii*) the placing of too heavy a load on the shoulders of fiscal policy in general, and of the central budget in particular; the difficulty here was aggravated by want of knowledge of the economic effects of the activities of public authorities, traceable partly to the absence of economically meaningful methods of presenting and keeping the public accounts; (*iv*) especially at first, too great a pre-occupation with internal plans to the neglect of the extreme precariousness of the foreign balance. Not all of these difficulties would necessarily occur again, or not all at the same time, although they must serve as warnings in any future attempt to establish a semi-planned economy. Our concern here is primarily with the third set of factors, although public finance has also a heavy responsibility to bear in other respects also.

One of the most important elements of inconsistency in post-war fiscal policy was between the restrictive policy for which the situation called (and which was on the whole genuinely attempted on the revenue side of the central budget), and the expansionary forces set loose by income redistribution through progressive taxation and the establishment of vast new social services. This was especially true of 'open-ended' expenditure, as the National Health Service and the food subsidies were at first, and as the Equalization grant to local authorities was throughout.[1] The economic situation called urgently for additional personal saving; everything—the reaction from war-time habits, the incidence of progressive taxation, the greater equalization of incomes by public expenditure, and the reduction of the need for private provision for the future due to the extended social security system—conspired to reduce it.

A further and most fundamental inconsistency arose between fiscal policy, which, as we have seen, at least in respect of taxation, attempted pretty steadily to be disinflationary, on the one side, and on the other credit policy, which, especially in the ultra-cheap money period (up to 1948)[2], was actively expansionary. A further lesson which can reasonably be drawn from this experience is that fiscal policy alone is neither comprehensive enough nor a strong enough instrument to bear the whole burden of stability control, at least if the tide is running strongly in an expansionary direction. This is largely because fiscal weapons tend to be themselves internally inconsistent in their effects: as income, profits, and wealth are swept away by progressive taxation, incentive to work and to enterprise tends to be lost also; as a budget surplus increases 'saving' in the public sector, the taxes by which it is secured tend to promote dis-saving in the private sector.

Inconsistent also was the neglect, not merely of the international balance in general, in contrast to the attention paid to internal planning, but also the effort made to stimulate exports in a situation in which unbalanced internal demand was continually pressing

[1] Analysed in Chapter IV. Established by the Local Government Act 1948.
[2] Analysed in Chapter VI.

up home consumption. This failure on the international side can perhaps be partly traced to the impunity with which—in very different circumstances—it had proved possible to neglect international repercussions in the compensatory finance of the '30s. One of the clearest lessons of 1945–51 is that for Britain international difficulties must be expected to be the rule rather than the exception.

Even, however, had these complicating factors not been present, the statistics behind planning were insufficient for their task, especially at first. There was little knowledge of the volume or location of investment, even within the public sector. Save possibly in industries dominated by a few giant firms, there was considerably less knowledge of the current activities and plans of private enterprise; this was especially true of the miscellaneous collection of 'other investment' whose magnitude could not accurately be measured, even *ex post*. The lack of knowledge of industry extended also to current operations. It is only in the most recent years that it has become possible to put together any sort of account of flows between the different parts of the industrial sector. In this respect Britain lagged far behind some other countries, where for want of good figures of income, it had always been necessary to build up national income estimates on the output side (which is of course the same thing looked at the other way round). For this purpose it had been necessary from an early stage to get adequate statistical information from firms; this was especially true in the United States.

The want of knowledge of the amount and direction of investment proved a severe handicap in implementing a stability policy in Britain, especially when the fuel crisis of 1947 made it imperative rapidly to cut down investment. These statistical lacunæ are, however, now steadily being filled, but the fact that investment plans are often drastically altered during implementation makes it unlikely that investment forecasts can ever attain a high degree of precision.

Perhaps even more serious from the point of view of national balance was the paucity of information concerning private saving, which could only be estimated as a residual, without independent check. This has implied that estimates for a particular year have often been substantially altered in a later year, thus upsetting the structure of the integrated national income account, and increasing the difficulties of forecast. This points to a more serious limitation of the entire method of planning for stability *via* estimates of the 'gap' between aggregate effective demand on resources and aggregate supplies available, as was at first attempted. Of later years much greater emphasis has been placed on tracing the flows of transactions, fundamentally of real goods and services, but of necessity measured in money flows, between the different economic sectors of the economy; as we have seen, this is the technique known by the statisticians as 'social accounting'.

All of these flows tend to be 'mixed', containing both current and investment items, the latter consisting both of stock changes and of fixed capital formation. These will have essentially different effects on the level of effective demand and on the supply of consumable goods. It is thus a fundamental necessity to be able to distinguish between current and capital flows. As a knowledge of these intersectoral relations improves it should become increasingly possible to give 'real' content to the money flows; showing the balance of demands for 'output' and the consequent demands for 'input' between one sector and another, and even between one firm and another. This type of 'input-output' analysis, as economists call it, should eventually provide a far firmer basis for forecasting than any yet available.

The extension of the coverage of policy from budget balance to national balance is a result both of the new social accounting technique and of the enlargement of the activities of the public sector. Like charity, however, statistical knowledge can best begin at home, and a priority for fiscal policy should be to adapt the system of public accounts so that they give a picture of the activities of public authorities which is economically meaningful, and will hence enable the public sector to take its correct place alongside of the other sectors of the economy. These, at least so far as concerns firms, of necessity already keep their accounts in a manner that is as economically meaningful as they know how to make it.

The need for the reform of government accounting was recognized by economists as soon as the new techniques of fiscal policy were put into practice; but the Treasury was naturally anxious that nothing should be done to disturb the system of accountability control, working, as we have seen, through the Gladstonian institution of central check of exclusively cash records of transactions. The need for reform was first realized at the official level by Sir Stafford Cripps when in his first budget (1948) he attempted a better distinction between current and capital items in order to isolate the former, on which the contribution of the central government to saving or dis-saving depends. Cripps's

'Alternative Classification' of the Budget accounts has since been annually presented; but although it is an improvement over the traditional form from the point of view which he had in mind, it pretends to be no more than a re-arrangement at the final stage, which is clearly an insufficient answer to the problem.

The problem of the adaptation of public accounting for modern purposes is somewhat technical, and we cannot do more here than indicate the lines of approach. It is desirable to do this, however, so that the factors at issue may be more widely appreciated. Broadly, there are now three uses to which we may need to put the accounts of the public sector: (*i*) There is first the traditional function of accountability control, or, as it was phrased in 1951 by the Committee on the Form of Government Accounts, an 'account of stewardship for the information of Parliament and as a guidance for future Votes'. (*ii*) There is the problem which Sir Stafford Cripps tried to solve, of estimating the true contribution of public authorities to saving or dis-saving. (*iii*) There is the social accounting problem of integrating government accounts with those of the other sectors of the economy, in order to draw up the complete accounts of the nation, necessary both from the point of view of planning internal stability and of international balance.

The traditional cash basis of accounts, and the control system which accompanied it, were evolved to suit a situation where the activities of the central government were primarily administrative. Where this was not so the system was recognized not to work well. For instance, the Public Accounts Committee laboured for decades to evolve a system which would give a truer record of stock and store changes in the defence departments. Nowadays, of course, the activities of public authorities are no longer predominantly administrative, and it is *prima facie* unlikely that this system of accounts would be appropriate for all their diverse activities. Even for purely administrative functions it is less than adequate in the sense that it provides a check only on accuracy, not on efficiency, in carrying out a particular task.

Nevertheless, the cash system is still not inappropriate for purely administrative functions, and is probably worth keeping, at least for the present for such services, from the point of view of accountability control. This would not preclude a re-classification of administrative activities so as to distinguish from the outset (and not merely at the final stage) between current and capital items,[1] and also between outlay which does, and which does not, exercise economic effects on home markets. Such a re-classification would go far to provide a true figure of central government saving or dis-saving; but it would also be necessary in certain cases to have estimates which would go beyond a cash basis, to what accountants call a 'receivable-payable' basis. An instance would be taxes assessed but not yet paid, which are allowed for in the commercial accounts of firms but not in the cash accounts of governments. Some progress in this direction has recently been made; by constant but gentle pressure, the Central Statistical Office is helping departments to think along social accounting lines.

All of this concerns the administrative departments. At the other extreme of public activities are those

---

[1] At this level capital items would take the form of gifts or loans to investing entities, for instance the Colonial Development Corporation or the Universities.

which are primarily economic, such as the trading operations of central departments and *a fortiori* the productive activities of the nationalized industries. There is no difficulty of principle here; it is agreed that economic entities should keep commercial accounts, which will give as meaningful an economic record of operations as can be devised, and which need no adjustment for social accounting purposes. In practice, however, a difficulty has been encountered over the trading operations of the central departments. Regarded as temporary, their accounts have never been separated in the Estimates from the administrative activities of the same departments. This is most unsatisfactory; the Ministry of Food in particular has in certain years changed its stocks by hundreds of million pounds, without one penny of these transactions appearing in the Budget, thus making havoc of the records of public saving or dis-saving.[1] The remedy for this lacuna is, however, near at hand, and was indeed recommended by the Committee on the Form of Government Accounts: to constitute departmental trading operations as separate public corporations, keeping full commercial accounts. Even if some of the activities should prove temporary the experience gained would be of great value on another occasion.

There remain, however, a number of miscellaneous public activities which do not fit neatly into either the administrative or the economic category, and for whom neither system of accounting is fully appropriate. These are departments or agencies whose activities,

[1] The fact that the C.S.O. does its best to account for these stock changes in the estimates of National Income and Expenditure is not really sufficient, since the two accounts relate to different years—financial and calendar—respectively.

while not in any ordinary sense economic, are yet engaged in producing goods or services in the course of which operation they make use of—and must maintain—capital assets, including both fixed equipment and stocks. Into this category fall on the one hand the roads and the Ministry of Works (responsible for all government buildings); on the other such organizations as the hospitals of the National Health Service, some of the activities of the defence departments (Royal Ordinance Factories and Naval Dockyards, for instance), and many of the activities of local authorities. For none of these is cash accounting adequate because it cannot make sense of investment activities; on the other hand, since there are no cash sales, out of which interest and depreciation would be covered, so that capital must be maintained out of the general tax pool, commercial accounting would not have its normal meaning.

For these departments a compromise solution must needs be sought, or perhaps a number of compromise solutions, since the activities are considerably diverse. There are, however, strong arguments for believing that a solution nearer commercial-type accounting would give better results than falling back on a cash record. For instance, commercial accounting applied to roads would facilitate the formation of a unified road plan based on economic considerations. The fact that it would be neither possible nor meaningful to 'value' the entire road system is irrelevant, since the cost of 'maintenance due' can readily be estimated, while proposed improvements can be weighed on a strictly economic basis of estimated cost set against estimated saving in transport delays. Again, the conduct of the Ministry of Works on a commercial basis, charging rents to government departments and in return maintaining the buildings in good repair, would almost certainly result in the provision of a better standard of accommodation by the 'landlord' and a more careful use of public property by the 'tenant'. This method is used with success in Sweden.

For the 'job performing' organizations, such as the hospitals or, say, local authority cleansing departments, it should seriously be considered whether some sort of 'unit costing' method could not be used as a check on efficiency.[1] This is near to what the Americans call 'performance budgeting' and has been recommended for the whole federal budget by the Commission on the Reform of the Executive.

Finally all these various sub-sector accounts within the public sector need to be knit into a single account for the whole public sector—the Committee on the Form of Government Accounts was most insistent on this and would like to have seen rough estimates at least available quarterly. Without this essential process of consolidation it is obvious that there will be much double counting of inter-governmental transactions (such as taxes paid by one authority to another) which will falsify the total reckoning.

The justification of these rather detailed reforms is the predominant role which public finance must henceforward play as an instrument of policy. Even if it should prove both practicable and desirable to restore credit policy to something of its former importance as an instrument of stability (a question on which

[1] For this also there is a precedent—in the Army Accounts, 1919–1925. A study of the record of this abortive experiment suggests that it was abandoned because it was attempted too suddenly and on too large a scale, not because it was inherently ineffective. In fact it was born out of due time.

we must touch in the next chapter), the size which public sectors have attained in modern economies and the subtleties of the fiscal instrument which modern economic analysis has revealed, alike assure that fiscal policy must in future be the senior partner.

M

Chapter VI

LOAN FINANCE AND DEBT MANAGEMENT

WHEN national governments cannot cover their expenditure requirements from taxation or other genuine current revenue, such as income from property, they must needs make use of some form of borrowing. National governments can always exercise this reserve power of borrowing because they have unlimited tax powers, unlike municipal governments which can in a sense go bankrupt if they overspend their incomes. Since it is certain that a national government can pay the interest on its debt out of tax revenue there will always be lenders to come forward unless and until the government loses the confidence of the public. Excessive borrowing will, however, tend to weaken the national currency on international markets, and it is by inflationary effects of this sort that trouble is most likely to arise from it.

Generally speaking, deficit finance on any substantial scale is, and should be, only necessary to finance major wars. It is inevitable that it should then be resorted to because without drawing on funds destined for the maintenance of capital assets as well as on current incomes, insufficient control over resources would be available to provide war material. In addition to war borrowing modern analysis has shown that some amount of borrowing may also be called for as part of a policy of compensatory finance. Debt which is accumulated either in fighting a war or in fighting a depression by general deficit finance is known as 'deadweight' since no tangible assets remain to balance it, although in the case of compensatory finance the net cost to the nation may well be smaller than allowing unemployment to continue.

Governments may also undertake borrowing of another type: to finance public investment; and this, as we have seen, is becoming an increasingly important call on the resources of the nation. Debts of this type will be matched by valuable assets, such as houses or power stations, which will produce part, perhaps the whole of the funds required to service the debt. They are thus of an essentially different character from deadweight debt. Nevertheless, the fact that the borrower is more or less the same in both cases, and must make use of similar channels of finance, implies that the problem of providing for public investment impinges on that of other borrowing and may act as an additional complication, especially in the market for long term capital.

It is evident from these considerations that problems of borrowing and debt management will be of increasing importance in the modern economy. The processes of borrowing and repayment, and of servicing the existing debt, have similar economic effects to the processes of taxation and public expenditure. Their effects therefore need to be considered along with those of other aspects of public finance; they cannot usefully be kept in a separate compartment.

The process of borrowing works in an expansionary direction because expenditure can be made, and additional incomes distributed, without any member of the public having to curtail his outlay, as he would have to do if the expenditure had been covered by taxation.

On the other hand, if the pressure on available funds is heavy the process of borrowing may tend to raise interest rates and hence set up some contractionary tendency. This result can indeed be counteracted by supplying the public with more liquid funds, most easily through the banking system; but that is merely another method of adding still further to the debt. *Mutatis mutandis* the process of repayment of public debt is normally contractionary; since a net repayment can only be financed by a budget surplus, more is taken in from taxpayers than is put out in real government expenditure. On the other hand many of the debt holders may re-invest their funds in similar securities, thus tending to lower interest rates and so to off-set the contractionary effects of repayment.

The effect of a given volume of borrowing or repayment will naturally vary with the economic situation. It will depend also on the type of debt and the channels through which it is raised. Generally speaking borrowing which involves the creation of money (printing additional notes, or, quantitatively now much more important, creating additional bank deposits) is the most expansionary. In this case the assets acquired by the public, being completely liquid, can be put to any desired use without loss—though here again the effect may differ according as the additional funds are made available to consumers who will probably spend them or to firms who may save them, at least in the first instance.

Other forms of borrowing can be arranged in descending order of expansionary effect as they approximate less and less nearly to the creation of money. In particular loans with only a short time to run before repayment (such as Treasury bills of any form of debt which is near maturity) are 'near money' or in bank terminology a 'quick asset'. Under modern conditions, however, techniques are available to the monetary authorities which tend to make these distinctions in the type of borrowing of less importance. When the monetary authorities are prepared, as they were during and immediately after the war both in this country and in the U.S.A., to buy back their own debt from the owners at fixed prices,[1] longer-term debt becomes virtually as liquid as short-term; indeed the Americans described the mechanism by which this was done as a process of 'monetizing' the debt.

In periods when the national debt is neither rapidly expanding nor contracting, but when there has recently been a large expansion (as after a major war), debt management is particularly important. Apart from any net repayment which may be possible from budget surpluses, there will all the time in such a period be a substantial and recurrent process of repayment and re-financing, as the efflux of time turns long-term debt into short and then into mature debt. As this process takes place what started as long-term debt, suitable for investment by trustees and similar institutions, becomes eventually a money-market asset, with consequent change of economic significance. Repayment and re-financing can within limits be adjusted to accelerate or retard this process, so that the policy implications of debt management during a period of this nature are hardly less important than during a period of active borrowing.

The art of debt management is concerned with the

---

[1] The process was much more informal in Britain than in the U.S.A., but in practice the result was similar. See below p. 173.

timing and the choice of the most appropriate type of
debt and channels for borrowing, repayment, or re-
financing; having regard to the needs of the economic
situation and the relative abundance of funds seeking
investments of different varieties. Judicious policy can
be made to serve both the cause of reducing the
budgetary charge of the debt service and the wider
interests of fiscal policy.

In Britain, deadweight debt, as has been indicated,
has only substantially increased as a result of major
wars. The permanent debt came into existence with
the Bank of England, whose primary purpose indeed
was to channel the savings of the City to finance the
war against Louis XIV. In 1697 the debt amounted to
£14·5 mn.; by the end of the war, in 1714, it had
reached £36 mn. The Napoleonic wars saw an expansion of the debt from £243 mn. to £834 mn.; this total
was reduced during the relatively peaceful years of
the nineteenth century, so that at the beginning of the
first world war the debt stood at only £649·7 mn. The
end saw it raised to £7831 mn. Again the second world
war carried it roughly from £7000 mn. to £23,000 mn.
and the reconstruction period to £25,000 mn. These
figures imply that in between the major wars there have
been long periods when there was little scope for active
debt management; this does not rule out that the
presence of the debt in the economy may have had
substantial economic effects.

As we have seen, the Victorians were much exercised
by the size of the debt and strove always to achieve
some regular annual repayment by means of a budget
surplus. This was mainly because they feared difficulty
in tapping the country's still limited supply of savings

in case of need. In fact the opportunities for public borrowing were limited, especially on short term, before the invention of the Treasury bill in 1877. That the Victorians were not more concerned with the effect of the annual interest charge is explained by the small dimensions to which it had been reduced by repayment and by a substantial conversion operation in 1889, which had established a large block of borrowing (known as Old Consols) on a $2\frac{3}{4}$ per cent. basis, automatically becoming $2\frac{1}{2}$ per cent. in 1902. In view of the troubles which the government got into over its borrowing policy in the first world war it was extremely fortunate that the Victorians bequeathed a debt problem of such modest dimensions.

On the other hand, although this was not expressly realized in the nineteenth century, the existence of a moderate public debt may be a considerable economic and financial convenience to a country. It provides a practically riskless security for investors, thus both encouraging the habit of saving and providing an extremely convenient collateral for 'venturing' on the part of the small firm. The existence of the debt and the debtor-creditor relation between the government and the banks which it implies, also gives the monetary authorities a means of credit control *via* the needs of financial institutions for liquid holdings of different types. Thus it can be argued that in principle the public debt is a beneficent and stabilizing influence in an economy. At least some of the instability of the American economy before 1914 can be ascribed to the small dimensions (and recurring almost complete extinction) of the federal debt, thus driving investors into less liquid and more risky depositories for their spare funds.

Although the volume of the public debt may thus exercise some influence in an economy, by and large the economic effects of the servicing of the debt are of much greater significance. If the payment of debt interest requires a transfer of incomes which is not negligible in relation to total incomes, it tends to exert a depressing effect in two ways. On the one hand the rentier debt holder receives a substantial income free of effort and may thus be deterred from activity; on the other the taxpayer must submit to higher, perhaps much higher rates than would otherwise be necessary, and this may have serious dis-incentive effects. Indeed it may be said that the real burden of the national debt is the cost of the high and progressive taxes which must be levied to service it.

The effect on rentiers' initiative however can easily be exaggerated; the majority of debt holders are not the 'idle rich' who might otherwise be induced to work, but institutions and others who may well have a real economic use for their debt holdings. In so far as surtax payers are large holders of debt, moreover, they largely provide their own interest payments, so long as debt interest forms part of taxable income. This it has always done—with a few negligible exceptions—in Britain. Since, however, in modern conditions the main debt holders are institutions paying income tax (if at all) only at the standard rate, the tax effect of the debt may in certain conditions be serious.

Here however another and most important consideration enters. Debt interest is fixed in money terms, but its burden depends on the real resources which have to be sacrificed in order to meet this monetary charge. If prices rise relatively to their level at the time when the debt was acquired the corresponding real resources lost will be less; a sizeable inflation can 'float off' even a large debt in a surprisingly short space of time, but of course it may have other, more evil, counteracting effects. On the other hand, if prices are likely to fall there is a real danger that the burden of the debt may become seriously depressing. It cannot be said with certainty what the critical relation between the debt interest and the national income would be, especially since, as we have seen, it depends to a considerable extent on the distribution of the debt and rates of progressive taxation. It would appear from experience, however, that 3 per cent. or 4 per cent. can be borne lightly while 7 per cent. or 8 per cent. sets up serious repercussions.

This point was reached and passed in the late 1920s and it is not surprising that at that time there was a considerable body of expert opinion in favour of a supreme effort to pay off a substantial portion of the capital (figures of £4000 mn. to £5000 mn. were mentioned) in order to reduce the annual burden. In view of his debt management policy in the 1940s [1] it is interesting to note that Dr. Dalton was among the most active supporters of a capital levy along these lines. In the event the situation was relieved within a few years not by repayment but by the conversion of a large portion of the interest from a 5 per cent. to a $3\frac{1}{2}$ per cent. basis. Since the means at the disposal of the government for the control of the price level are now very much greater than they were in the 1920s it is probable that this particular embarrassment of the national debt is unlikely to recur with much violence.

It should not therefore lightly be concluded, as has been argued in some quarters, that an internal debt

[1] See below pp. 201 ff.

can never constitute a burden on an economy; it depends essentially on the net tax burden to which it gives rise. Other things being equal this depends on the rate of interest that has been offered to lenders when the debt was acquired, and this in turn depends largely on policy management, including the channels of finance which are selected. Thus a tax charge of under £250 mn. sustained a debt of over £23,000 mn. in 1946 while in 1926 £318 mn. was required to service a debt of under £8000 mn. In no aspect of debt policy have such great alterations taken place over the present generation than in the availability of different channels of finance.

In early times budget deficits were mainly covered by an increase in the supply of money, at first by debasing the coinage (making more pennies out of a given supply of metal), later, especially in the Napoleonic wars, by Ways and Means advances from the Bank of England, leading to the printing of additional notes. There was indeed from the sixteenth century some long-term lending to the government, but most of this should more properly be regarded as a substitute for income tax, which was as yet beyond the powers of the administration; the loans were not normally repaid or serviced. Elizabeth I raised long-term loans to finance her wars, but in the Netherlands, where the supply of savings had developed further than in England.

After the establishment of the Bank of England long-term lending to the government in times of emergency became generally popular, providing at the time one of the few channels for liquid investment. There was, however, continual apprehension at 'resort to the printing press' which represented the main channel of short-term borrowing. To some extent this fear, and the theory of inflation on which it was based (that prices would rise more or less proportionately to the increase in the circulation), was due to a misapprehension. The basic cause of inflation in wartime is the additional incomes generated by government spending, the increase in the circulation being merely an inevitable adjustment to this situation. This concern at the prospect of an increase in the note circulation endured unabated into the first world war, although by then it should have been evident that changes in the volume of bank deposits were of much greater quantitative importance, and that the significance of these would be affected not only by their volume but by the propensity of their owners to spend them or to keep them in liquid form. This apprehension was responsible, as we shall see, for a heavy emphasis on long-term borrowing to which the high cost of the 1914–18 debt was largely due.

The first significant step in improving the opportunities for public borrowing after the establishment of the Bank of England in 1694 was the invention of the Treasury bill in 1877. The importance of this device (and this was specifically the intention of Bagehot, its inventor) was that it fitted in exactly to the established machinery of the London Money Market. The commercial bill was then, at one and the same time, the principal means of short-term lending to finance international trade, the chief repository of the commercial banks for their short-term funds and the stock-in-trade of the discount market. Save for the absence of the risk attaching to a commercial transaction, the Treasury bill fulfilled exactly these requirements both for the banks and the discount houses. Up to 1914 however—largely owing to the absence of any great need for short-term public borrowing—the Treasury bill was hardly used except to cover a temporary deficit in anticipation of the collection of revenue. £13 mn. was considered a large supply of Treasuries and this was negligible in relation to the supply of trade bills, estimated at over £500 mn. It was with the first world war that the real usefulness of the Treasury bill first became apparent.

The borrowing of the first world war—percentage-wise even more striking than that of the second—at one stroke revolutionized the position of the public debt in the economy. Henceforward the Treasury bill dominated the money market, while the enormous volume of medium and longer-term debt largely determined conditions in the capital market. Debt management became a matter of national balance, not merely of budgetary convenience.

When the process of borrowing was complete (as recorded for instance in the Financial Statement of 1921) the volume of Treasury bills was roughly £1250 mn. while the volume of trade bills never recovered to more than about two thirds of its pre-war volume, representing of course a much smaller turnover of real transactions. Of fully as great importance was the creation during the war of a new category of safe investments in the form of over £2000 mn. of medium-term government debt, having a life of from one to five years at the end of the war. This medium-term debt formed an effective bridge between the short-term and long-term investments such as had never before existed. Significantly it gave rise to a new integration of the interest rate structure, since switching from one to another type of safe investment became a simple matter. In addition to these stood the even larger volume of long-term debt, with ten years or more to run, providing typical capital market assets.

Although it was not until the 1930s that the significance of the revolution which had taken place, both in the position of the public debt in the economy and, as a consequence, in the future operations of the banks and discount houses, was fully realized either by the Treasury or by the financial institutions themselves, it was inevitable from this point that the real control of money and credit policy should pass from the Bank of England to the Treasury, and thus become largely a function of debt management.

The borrowing of the first world war was an immense and unprecedented effort, comparable in importance, though far greater in magnitude, to the efforts which two centuries previously had led to the establishment of the Bank of England and the consequent victory of the arms of England and the Netherlands over the seemingly overwhelming power of Louis XIV. The process of borrowing from 1914 to 1919 was fully successful in the sense that the government never went short of funds or found itself in serious difficulty. In the light of more recently acquired expertise in borrowing and debt management, however, it can be seen that the methods used were often clumsy and wasteful; they left an aftermath of awkwardness which dogged the country's finances throughout the 1920s. The authorities assumed that England was an open economy in war as in normal times, and that consequently they must give first attention to the foreign balance even to the point of attracting American funds by offering very favourable rates of interest. This was only partly true; in practice it proved quite simple to peg the external value of the pound. Moreover, internally, the fact that the opportunities of doing other things with the additional incomes of wartime than lend to the government were strictly circumscribed, was never fully taken advantage of in arranging the channels of borrowing. On the contrary the government was perpetually haunted by the fear of running short of funds.

This apprehension was largely misplaced, but was partly justified by the fact that without an established tradition of borrowing more or less continuously in small blocks of medium-term debt, the only choice open was either floating debt, too great an expansion of which was felt to be inflationary, or blocks of long-term war loans. The successive war loans were large relatively to the market and consequently hard for it to digest. On each occasion the banks created enormous additional credit in order to ensure the success of the loan, while the Treasury itself had but indifferent means of controlling the operations of the banks, although from time to time it did apparently borrow bank cash from the Bank of England. (It will be remembered that the great bank amalgamations from which in the 1920s the 'Big Five' emerged had not yet taken place; so that bank management was much more dispersed than it afterwards became.)

To ensure the success of the issues as much as to attract foreign balances, each successive war loan was floated at a rate which was not only more favourable to lenders than those of its predecessors, but was on each occasion criticized in the City for over-generosity. This was clearly wasteful. More serious than this were the privileges offered to subscribers, such as (in some cases) freedom from taxation at the source, and above all the right, known as 'covenanted benefit', of transferring from one loan to other more favourable issues. By this means the cost of the whole long-term debt rose *pari passu* with interest rates, and in the later loans conversions tended heavily to exceed new subscriptions. From this point of view the most attractive issue to investors was the 5 per cent. war loan of 1917 (issued at 95), which accumulated £837 mn. of new subscriptions and £1231 mn. of conversions, thus building an exceptionally large block of debt all maturing in 1929–32. Once this became eligible for repayment it swamped the market with an enormous block of short-term funds and it was only when (in 1932) it finally became possible to deal with the problem (partly by conversion and partly by repayment) that conditions in the money market could be restored to normal.

Owing to the complications in which they found themselves in respect of the long-term loans the government came to rely very heavily on Ways and Means advances from the Bank of England and on expanded issues of Treasury bills. By this means the Market was supplied with two to three times as much liquid resources as they had been accustomed to. Towards the end of the war bills were issued 'on tap' at fixed rates to all who applied for them. As developed later the device of 'continuous borrowing'—of which this was an example—proved a most useful method which was much used in the second world war and reconstruction period. In the absence of market controls other than through the rate of discount (nullified by issue through the tap) the resulting liquidity proved embarrassing to the authorities. It was not until 1926 that the Treasury felt secure enough to return to the pre-war method of issuing Treasury bills only through the tender; from that time the volume was steadily reduced, settling down at a seasonal level of £550–£600 mn. Even at that level the market was rather excessively well supplied, taking into account the effect of the partial revival of trade bills and of the rapidly maturing longer-term war debt.

The method of continuous borrowing was also applied to Savings Certificates, tapping for the first time the current savings of the small investor, transformed by the war into a modest capitalist. Something very similar was also applied in the later stages of the war by means of small and frequent issues of medium-term bonds. Thus by the end of the war the Treasury had evolved a technique of borrowing which took advantage of a much wider and more varied demand for securities than had previously been thought to exist. In so doing the gaps in the 'spectrum' of interest rates were gradually closed, so that the gradation from rate to rate and maturity to maturity became almost continuous. This greatly increased the possibilities of control through the natural reaction of arbitrage by professional operators to pressure applied at one point or another; but the use of this new device still remained for the future. In one respect the borrowing of the first world war was considerably more prudent than that of the second: scrupulous care was taken not to accumulate overseas debt in excess of the debts owed to Britain. The greater spatial limitation of the range of war operations of course made this easier than in the 1940s.

The chief problems of debt management in the 1920s were concerned with the digestion of the excess liquidity of the Money Market, and (which was really the other side of the same problem) the removal of the large block of 5 per cent. war loan from the purview of the Market. These problems need not have been at all as intractable as they proved but for the return to the gold standard at the pre-war parity in 1925. At this level of the pound it never proved possible for Britain to accumulate through her exports sufficient international reserves to maintain parity in a normal manner; hence she came to rely more and more on the presence of foreign funds in London, on some occasions even to balance her current payments account. In order to ensure the continuance of this short-term foreign lending it was necessary to offer on bills and bank deposits rates of interest that would successfully compete with other financial centres, especially New York. This implied the maintenance of a Bank Rate which after 1925 was never less than $4\frac{1}{2}$ per cent., with $2\frac{1}{2}$ per cent. consols yielding $4\frac{1}{2}$ per cent. and firms having to offer 6 per cent. or more on good industrial debentures.

Rates such as these inevitably affected the level of employment and restricted the growth of new investment. Their artificiality was evident from the difficulty experienced in making Bank Rate effective. Market rates repeatedly tended to slip down to a level which might prove unattractive to the foreign balances. In the narrow sense of a monetary manœuvre however, this policy succeeded until the universal crash of 1931, but it cannot be doubted that it contributed to the high level of unemployment which had persisted steadily from the post-war slump of 1921. It was suggested that Bank Rate was being deliberately used to force a lower price and wage structure on the economy; this would indeed have been consistent with the logic of the Bank Rate technique but would have been without precedent in any previous use of the machinery.

If, however, arguments of this type played any substantial part in policy it was not followed consistently, either by the Chancellors, who not only failed to secure effective budget surpluses in support of monetary restriction but allowed the Unemployment Fund to run into substantial deficit; or even by the Bank, which on a number of occasions replenished the resources of the Market with additional credit after they had been depleted by the withdrawal of foreign balances. In the meantime with the steady fall in prices of the later '20s the burden of the debt service was rising to intolerable levels. Thus in the first period after the fortunes of war had supplied the Treasury with important new tools of control it did not prove possible to put them to any useful purpose.

Once the gold standard had been abandoned, in September 1931, the requirements of the interest rate situation changed abruptly, and with it the problems of debt management. With restored control over the internal market situation the tools of modern monetary and debt management technique began rapidly to take shape. The turning point in all this was the Great Conversion of the large block of 5 per cent. war loan on to a $3\frac{1}{2}$ per cent. basis, carried through in the summer of 1932. It is significant that the $3\frac{1}{2}$ per cent. rate was considerably lower than that ruling in the market when the operation was set on foot. Once, however, the $3\frac{1}{2}$ per cent. rate could be captured and confirmed, the whole interest rate structure quickly fell into line. Not only this block of war loan, but a number of other high-yielding public loans were converted, local authority loans and industrial debentures also benefited from the changed conditions.

The mechanics of the Great Conversion need not detain us; they were compounded of a large increase in market and bank liquidity brought about by open market purchases, a welcome return of foreign balances to London (now regarded as the safest place in a crumbling world), and a great deal of rather crude propaganda, including commissions for all and sundry who could claim to have secured conversions. The cost of all this to the taxpayer was nearly £30 mn. The sledgehammer, however, cracked the nut without difficulty; once the dam had been broken the downward pressure of market forces in deepening depression was sufficient to maintain low interest rates, with little, if any, further effort on the part of the authorities.

The significant fact about the Great Conversion was that it pointed the way to the use of debt management as a controllable instrument of policy. The authorities had striven to convert the war loan primarily in the interests of budget economy; with that stroke they created cheap money and created it as the result of a fiscal rather than a merely monetary manœuvre. Within a few years, when the beneficent stimulus of low interest rates on the level of activity became apparent, the government was explicitly claiming responsibility for the improvement.

In the course of the 1930s two further instruments of modern debt management were evolved, both full of presage for the future. The first was the use of internal government balances as a repository for longer term issues (required in the course of re-financing the war debt) which were either held in portfolio or perhaps fed gradually to the market in accordance with its digestive capacity. Secondly came the greatly extended use of an obscure (and hence not

immediately recognizable) small Discount House for
government business so that this 'Special Buyer' (later
to attain great notoriety) could operate inconspicuously
to ease temporary jams and stringencies in the Market.
By this means interest rates could be kept from rising
in the short run, while 'departmental intervention' of
the first type kept them smoothly at low levels in the
longer run.

In a sense neither technique was new in principle.
Gladstone had remarked with extraordinary prescience
that the government was like a gigantic bank, since
there were always some departments with funds
seeking investment as well as others requiring funds.
In his day the important agency for the investment of
funds was the Office of the Commissioners of the
National Debt who were responsible for the management of the funds of the Trustee (and later the Post
Office) Savings Banks. Gladstone envisaged the N.D.C.
funds as primarily a means of guaranteeing net national
debt repayment because they would be less easy to raid
when invested in terminable annuities than a sinking
fund, which could be suspended at the will of Parliament. From time to time N.D.C. funds are still used
for the purchase of annuities, but their more important
work now is in connection with the launching and not
the repayment of loans. It is in this role that they
attained notoriety in the Dalton era as 'The Public
Stag'.

In the early 1930s, owing to the severity of the
depression, savings bank funds were at an abnormally
low ebb, so that opportunities for departmental intervention of the traditional type were less than usually
good. Fortune, however, placed in the hands of the
authorities a new source of internal lending which

proved of inestimable advantage for debt management throughout the '30s. This was the Exchange Equalization Account or Exchange Fund, established in 1932 on the abandonment of the gold standard, in order to buy up foreign balances seeking investment in London (both with the purpose of insulating the British economy from their vagaries and of maintaining sterling at the chosen international parity). The Exchange Fund was able to serve debt management in this way because it operated with non-market Treasury bills, issued to it 'through the tap', with which it traded in foreign exchange and gold. Funds not currently required for these operations could take over bills from other departments, leaving them free to take up long-term stock, while if the Exchange Fund became so choked with gold that it could no longer absorb more bills (as happened on more than one occasion) its gold could always be sold to the Bank of England against securities.

During the 1930s these 'extra-budgetary funds' were used in the interests of debt management in two ways: the first relating to the market rate of discount on bills, the second to longer-term, capital market rates. The technique of the first of these methods was for the Treasury to 'ration' the volume of bills offered for tender to the Market to such an amount as would balance the foreseeable demand at a very low rate of interest, the government satisfying its remaining needs through internal bills issued to 'the departments' through the tap. Longer-term rates on new loans (representing recurrent instalments of re-financing the war debt) could be controlled, although less certainly, by 'the departments' taking up initially as much of the new loan as would ensure its success at a low rate of interest, and feeding these holdings gradually to investors (mainly financial institutions and above all the banks) as their appetite demanded. If financial institutions were reluctant lenders the banks could be supplied with so much liquid funds as would upset their structure of assets until the normal ratio of 'quick assets' to 'investments' was restored by the acquisition of further long-term investments. The authorities were assisted in this policy by the fact that the banks were coming more and more to rely on a liquidity criterion defined in terms of a ratio of total quick assets, including cash, short loans and bills, to deposits, rather than the traditional liquidity ratio of cash alone to deposits.

Largely as a result of the use of these new devices, bill rates in the 1930s were kept at the unprecedently low level of well under 1 per cent. (see Chart III), while the long-term rate (represented by the yield on $2\frac{1}{2}$ per cent. 'Old' Consols), which had fallen to $3\frac{1}{2}$ per cent. in 1932, reached about $2\frac{3}{4}$ per cent. in 1935 and did not return to the 3 per cent. level until 1937, when the shadow of the second world war began to fall across the path of the City. These rates were substantially lower than had been experienced since the 1890s, especially on the floating and shorter-term debt. Important as the new techniques were, however, it must be emphasized that conditions in the 1930s were quite exceptionally favourable for the maintenance of low rates. Investment demand was at a low ebb, while owing to the continued influx of foreign balances (up to 1937–8) and the operations of the Exchange Fund, the British monetary economy was so insulated as to assume many of the characteristics of a closed economy. In this situation additional liquidity could be repeatedly injected to the banks without embarrassing the foreign balance.

The Treasury was thus able to carry out its chosen course of debt management with a minimum of active pressure. Further, although there was no formal control of capital issues, in fact those home issues over which the Treasury had some natural influence, such as the loans of local authorities, were carefully steered and timed so as to avoid awkward pressure on the stock exchange. Indeed, except at first, little psychological pressure was exerted, beyond a repeated extolling of the virtues of cheap money. When in 1937–38 the tide turned and the exchanges moved against Britain, interest rates rose only slowly; instead the Exchange Fund steadily disgorged its gold through 1938. Thus, on the eve of the second world war the level of interest rates was still low and substantially more favourable for renewed borrowing than it had been in 1914. In spite of this (on the whole) passive attitude of the authorities in the later 1930s, by the outbreak of war the revolution in monetary management had been firmly consolidated. Already by 1936, ten years before nationalization, the Governor of the Bank of England was assuring Ministers that 'they will find us [the Bank Court] at all times as willing with goodwill and loyalty to do what they direct as though we were under legal compulsion'.[1]

From this point it was necessary for the government, implicitly if not explicitly, to accept responsibility for credit control through the management of its debt. To the economic effects of the budget surplus or deficit were superimposed the effects of interest rate

[1] Mansion House Speech, 6 October 1936.

policy. The direct fruits of this change were not fully matured until after the end of the second world war, but soon after its beginning a new and purposive sense of control could be perceived in debt policy. This was very largely traceable to the influence and even the physical presence of Keynes at the Treasury, anxious to use to the full the new opportunities which were now open. As we have seen, within a few months of the beginning of the war the recipe for an over-all fiscal policy based on national income estimates had already been expounded. To accompany this fiscal policy there was an appropriate debt policy based on a continuation of the low interest rates of the 1930s, thus promoting on the monetary side that stability of prices which would be secured on the fiscal side by high income taxes, consumers' subsidies and rationing. The social objective of continuing the process of the 'euthanasia of the rentier' (in Keynes' famous phrase) would serve also to further the budgetary objective of minimizing the debt charge.

The policy which governed the loan operations of the '3½ per cent. war' (actually the average rate of interest on the roughly £14,000 mn. of new borrowing which took place between 1939 and 1945 was considerably lower than this) can be summarized in a phrase as 'glutting a closed economy with cash', or in other words supplying the public, whether individuals, firms, or financial institutions, with sufficient liquid funds to satisfy completely their every demand. This simple phrase, however, does no justice to the ingenuity with which debt policy ministered to these diverse demands so that as the war progressed, contrary to all precedent, interest rates actually fell, while at the same time policy was so geared as effectively to hold in check the vast inflationary potential of the monetary expansion.

As compared with the borrowing policy of the first world war the conspicuous developments between 1939 and 1945 were four: first comes the greatly extended use of continuous borrowing which (as we have seen) was evolved—or perhaps, more accurately, stumbled upon—only in the closing stages of the first world war. Continuous borrowing now touched the public both through savings certificates, always on offer, and through periodic 'flowing of the tap' for longer-term bonds. The banks were made subject to weekly demands on their funds through the Treasury Deposit Receipt, a six-month security instituted soon after Dunkirk. The Money Market received its weekly ration of Treasury bills at a pegged rate only one half per cent. above that of the 1930s. Finally (from early in 1941) business firms were offered Tax Reserve Certificates for the investment of their idle funds at a 1 per cent. rate of interest and the right to charge the certificates as 'capital employed in the business' for Excess Profits Tax.

Secondly, these methods of borrowing were not merely effective in expanding the government's control over resources without resorting to formal issues of war debt; they were also deliberately designed to reduce the inflationary potential by limiting the rise in bank deposits. From this point of view the T.D.R. was by far the more important; not only was there a much larger volume (£1859 mn. was outstanding in March 1945 as against £683 mn. of T.R.Cs.), but it constituted a direct tie-up of bank money for six months at a time, and unlike the Treasury bill was not discountable. In view of this rigidity large demands on the banks for T.D.Rs. might indeed have put them in an embarrassing position, but so long as net new borrowing was going on this was avoided by giving them the right of pre-encashment against subscriptions to new loans. After the war when this safety valve no longer operated the use of the T.D.R. was gradually reduced.

Thirdly, borrowing policy in the second world war differed notably from that of the first in respect of the new direct relations which were established not only between the authorities and the money market institutions (with whom indeed they had all along been in contact through Treasury bill issues and discounting facilities), but also with the commercial banks with whom the Bank of England had had no direct contacts since early in the nineteenth century. In the 1930s the exceedingly low rate of discount on bills had already caused the discount houses to enter the better paying short bond market; their slender capitalization, however, implied that this new source of profit could only be indulged in with caution. With the special conditions of wartime this process became much less risky and the discount houses quickly became a regular and important depository for bonds as well as bills.

In addition to direct contact with the banks through the T.D.R. system the monetary authorities also occasionally sold bills direct to the banks, contrary to the convention established before the war that the banks would only acquire their bills at second hand from the discount houses; and on occasions they also bought bills back from the banks. The limitation of bank advances to firms engaged on government contracts further strengthened the contacts between the Treasury and the banks.

The lynch-pin of the whole system of control of

monetary institutions was the 'Special Buyer' who with the government broker was always at hand, not only to smooth out kinks and prevent jars as he had done in the 1930s, but now standing ready to buy indefinite amounts of government securities at fixed prices. Thus effective liquidity of all public debt, long or short, was assured; the normal distinctions in yield between quick assets, shorts and long-term loans virtually disappeared. This was the main explanation of the steady fall of long-term rates (greater relatively to short rates which had less far to fall) which was experienced as the war progressed.

Finally, behind the special agencies, for direct operation on longer-term issues stood the 'departments' with their extra budgetary funds waiting for investment in new issues, for eventual disposal to the public as opportunity offered, exactly as they had done in the 1930s but on a much more extended scale. The composition of the funds had now changed somewhat: the Exchange Fund was no longer useable, but enormous new accumulations were reaching the National Debt Commissioners on Savings Bank and similar accounts, while the Unemployment Insurance fund was also steadily growing. The National Debt Commissioners were able to use their funds in part to keep down the volume of Treasury bills by investing in terminable annuities, exactly in the Gladstone manner. The longer-term tap issues were in part designed to keep down the volume of bank deposits, and in part served as a means of tying up the funds of firms and individuals more securely than if they had been left in bank deposits, or even invested in savings certificates—although the terms of interest and repayment of these were specially geared to encourage long holding.

The tap loans were roughly divided into two classes: the shorter National War Bonds, maturing in the middle 1950s, having mainly an institutional (or at least non-personal) appeal, and the longer Savings Bonds maturing after 1955, designed primarily to attract personal savings. Loan efforts were concentrated in a series of enormous savings drives held every spring of the war: 'Warships' in 1942, 'Wings for Victory' in 1943, 'Salute the Soldier' in 1944 and finally 'Thanksgiving' when it was all over. These were accompanied by every psychological pressure that central or local ingenuity could devise. Towns were encouraged to believe that they were actually buying destroyers, or spitfires, as the case might be, and competition between neighbouring centres ran high. This high pressure salesmanship can be regarded as a more sophisticated—and much more economical, because largely voluntary—development of the salesmanship of the Great Conversion of 1932. Similar methods were to be used with even greater intensity during the Dalton era. Although the banks subscribed heavily to the tap loans as they had done to the big war loans of the first world war, they were so much more tightly controlled that hardly any additional inflationary pressure was thus generated.

By these means the entire process of war borrowing was carried through with the utmost smoothness, and a debt more than twice as large as that of the first world war raised at the cost of only a moderate rise in the debt charge (from 4·6 per cent. in 1938 to 6·2 per cent. of the national income in 1945). Moreover, it was well distributed as to maturities, so as to cater for every investment demand; great care was taken to avoid any concentration such as the £2000 mn. of 1917 War Loan which had overhung the market so long. Further, as we have seen, so far from there being any rise in interest rates as the war progressed, rates tended to fall, especially the long-term rate; only the market rate of discount, at 1 per cent., stood substantially above the level of the 1930s, but this was still low in relation to previous experience.

Only in respect of external borrowing was the situation more unfavourable than in the 1914–18 war. Although there were no formal external loans, such as there had been in the American market in the 1914–18 war, by the end of the war some £4000 mn. of sterling balances were held abroad, mainly by Commonwealth countries and about half on Indian account. As a consequence London found itself once more in the position of maintaining a precarious international balance only with the aid of outside deposits. The most serious aspect of the sterling balances was, however, economic rather than financial. The necessity to honour at least some proportion immediately in the form of 'unrequited' exports was felt as a drag on industrial reconstruction and an obstacle in the way of dollar-earning exports. It was not until 1950 that the balances were reduced to manageable proportions.

The end of hostilities did not see the end of new borrowing. Deficits on the current budget were experienced up to 1947, while investment needs, especially in local authority housing and later for the process of industrial nationalization, led to over-all budget deficits in all years except 1949 and 1950. While, as we saw in the last chapter, the current surplus or deficit on a well-arranged budget account is the best available measure of the contribution of the central government to saving or dis-saving, the apparent new borrowing in any year is only very loosely related to the recorded deficit; this is mainly due to the enormous variety in the channels of borrowing which can now be used. Table 12 attempts to illustrate this by showing the Central Statistical Office estimates of the true deficit (or surplus) in the central government account, set against the manner in which the deficit was financed.

Three points stand out clearly: first the relatively unimportant part played by government borrowing in the normal sense of an appeal to the public for funds; second the great importance of overseas funds in balancing the account, and hence in containing inflation, and thirdly the relatively great importance of the finance through 'government agencies'. It should be especially noted moreover that the account is seriously deficient in the record of these; in particular every increase in the note issue is matched by an equivalent increase in public debt held by the Issue Department of the Bank of England; it is a serious deficiency in our means of analysing debt management that no information is available of the distribution of securities thus held internally. Perhaps the most interesting aspect of the account thus presented is to emphasize the devious ways and complications of modern deficit financing and debt management, and as a result the many paths open to an ingenious Chancellor.

Although new borrowing continued well after the end of hostilities the predominant problem of the reconstruction period was, as it had been in the 1920s, that of re-financing and debt management. In the 1940s it was not (at least on the surface) a case of striving against odds to get the Money Market back into a manageable condition and to secure reasonably low rates of interest; rather the Chancellor, Dr. Dalton,

TABLE 12

The Central Government Deficit and its Finance
(£mn.)   (Calendar Years)
Source: National Income and Expenditure White Papers

	1938	1940	1942	1944	1946	1948	1950
Surplus (+) Deficit (−) on Current Account	− 123	− 2169	− 2972	− 2987	− 1024	310	481
1. *Finance through Government Agencies*							
Social Insurance Funds	− 1	33	86	77	81	115	169
Local Loans Fund	− 3	2	7	8	− 53	− 9	− 5
Other Extra-budgetary	264	614	6	− 87	− 203	84	− 508
Less Sinking Funds	− 11	− 12	− 13	− 16	− 17	− 23	− 19
Total Government Agencies	249	637	86	− 18	− 192	167	− 363
2. *Borrowing in the U.K.*							
National Savings	4	286	600	702	525	36	− 10
Other Public Issues (net)	73	567	1047	896	− 2	− 305	− 316
Increase in Note Issue	10	50	170	150	50	− 125	25
Increase in Market Treasury bills	− 189	129	151	537	321	− 199	661
T.D.R.s (net)	..	338	155	394	40	109	− 347
T.R.Cs	..	..	453	113	− 132	− 23	39
Total in the U.K.	− 102	1370	2576	2792	802	− 629	52
3. *Receipts from Abroad*							
Loans and Gifts	..	..	167	− 24	241	324	81
Sales of Stores, etc.	..	..	..	..	201	96	29
Total from Abroad	..	..	167	− 24	442	420	110

Notes to Table 12

1. These estimates (for the Calendar Year) cannot be precisely reconciled with those of the Financial Statement (for the Financial Year); they are also subject to qualification (see Chapter V) in respect of a number of items which determine the amount of the surplus or deficit. Further, they are not fully adjusted for stock changes and capital maintenance charges, nor for gold movements.

2. The official list of government agencies (here given) is incomplete; in particular the important contribution of the Issue Department of the Bank of England is omitted.

3. Some of the items from abroad do not necessarily affect the position in this country; further the list is incomplete since short-term lending by foreigners through bank deposits and holdings of Treasury Bills cannot be isolated.

appeared to be in the position of holding the markets in his hand and working his will upon them for a particular defined purpose: the reduction of interest rates to levels still lower than those to which the techniques of war borrowing had brought them.

The ulterior purpose of this policy would seem to have been mainly a minimization of the budgetary debt charge. It will be recalled that Dr. Dalton had in the 1920s been particularly impressed with the possibility that debt interest might be a serious competitor with expenditure on the social services, notwithstanding the extent to which debt-holders provided through their taxes their own interest payments. In addition to this personal idiosyncrasy stood the general belief (due to Keynes, and now held even more strongly by the Labour than by the Conservative party) that low rates of interest would be necessary to help reconstruction and to maintain full employment in what was misread (not only in Britain but also in the U.S.A.) as a potentially deflationary situation.

It was not until November 1951 that after an interval of twenty years a gradual return to the use of monetary policy in support of fiscal control was put into operation. Up to that time debt management exhibited a further intensification of all the methods used during the war, and for the most part, as we have seen, evolved during the 1930s. Of special importance were the devices of 'departmental intervention' and the operations of the Special Buyer. By far the most interesting years are those of the Dalton 'ultra-cheap money' experiment, which lasted from the autumn of 1945 to the autumn of 1947, with special intensity throughout the year 1946. Chart IV indicates the

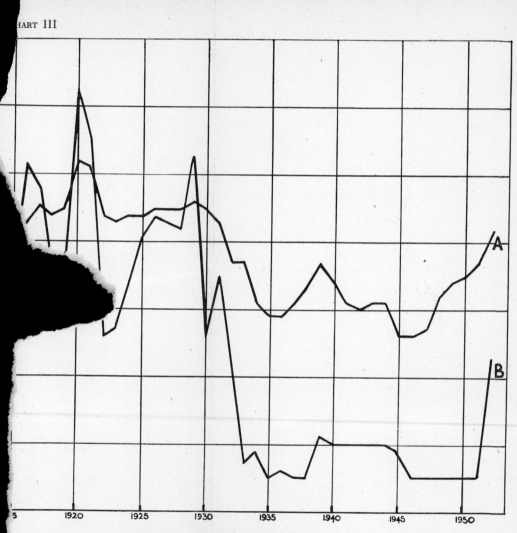

1920   1925   1930   1935   1940   1945   1950

B = Discount on Three Months Bills.

CHART IV

THE COURSE OF INTEREST RATES: 1945–53 (MONTHLY AVERAGES).

A = Yield on 2½ per cent. Consols.   B = Yield on Short-dated Securities.
C = Discount on Treasury Bills.

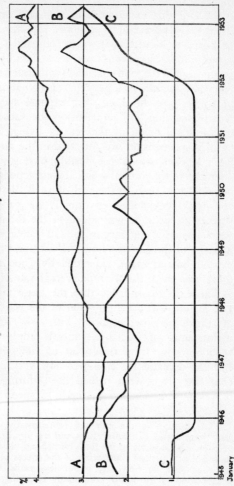

success of this experiment in terms of interest rate levels.[1] To appreciate its economic significance it must be borne in mind that it was accompanied by a large upsurge in social expenditure, as well as by a steadily mounting bill for food subsidies (which as we have seen reached £400 mn. or 4 per cent. of the national income in 1947); both of these were expansionary in effect notwithstanding any contribution the subsidies made to the stabilization of the cost of living. The result of all this expansion was reflected in the movement of bank deposits, which rose steadily, paying scarcely any attention to the normal seasonal contractions, from the beginning of 1946 to the end of 1948. Between 1938 and 1945 they had risen broadly by £2000 mn.; a further £2000 mn. was added in the three following years. Between January 1946 and January 1947 the deposits of the eleven Clearing Banks, as a clear result of debt management, expanded by £900 mn., or at more than twice the wartime average rate of growth.

These figures indicate that the basic technique of Dr. Dalton was a continuation of the wartime recipe of 'glutting a closed economy with cash', for the strict maintenance of exchange controls implied that the economy was, from this point of view, still closed. But the demand for cash was now very different in character from what it had been during the war: it was now a demand for cash to spend or invest,

---

[1] In addition to the accepted representatives of 'short' and 'long' rates (Treasury Bills and 2½ per cent. Consols respectively), a series of medium term bond yields has been included as a further illustration of the effects of the Dalton technique. It is, however, much less reliable since the composition is inevitably continually changing, and yields may be influenced by temporary variations in supply as well as by debt management policy.

and most emphatically not to save. Although the volume of savings certificates continued to rise slowly until 1948, Tax Reserve Certificates began to decline immediately on the close of hostilities. Hence the forcing down of interest rates through credit expansion carried with it a very much greater inflationary potential than the same operation carried through in war conditions. As *The Economist* put the matter at the end of 1946, 'Mr. Dalton has littered the British economy with dry inflationary paper'.[1]

That the net result was not more inflationary than in fact it proved was due primarily to three causes: first the maintenance of wartime levels of taxation and many of the wartime direct controls; secondly the tight hold on the stock exchange maintained through the operations of the Capital Issues Committee in respect of new issues, and even more important the limitation of carry-over from account to account, thus preventing the City from building up an adverse position and indeed forcing it to dance to the Chancellor's tune for many months; thirdly, and perhaps most important of all, the anti-inflationary 'assistance' of the adverse balance of payments, balanced by foreign aid.

Apart from the process of credit creation, the Dalton technique for reducing interest rates was a compound of extremely sensitive technical controls and of the psychological weapon. Those interest rates which were directly under Treasury control were lowered by simple announcement: the T.D.R. rate was reduced from $1\frac{1}{8}$ per cent. to $\frac{5}{8}$ per cent., and the discount rate on Treasury bills from 1 per cent. to $\frac{1}{2}$ per cent. already in October 1945; in April 1946 the T.R.C. rate was dropped from 1 per cent. to $\frac{3}{4}$ per cent., and finally,

[1] *The Economist*, 12 October 1946.

but at a considerably later date, the rate offered on savings certificates suffered a similar fate. This last reduction, however, was not an operative factor in the downward pressure on rates, but rather a half reluctant adjustment to the new conditions which had been secured.

In accordance with precedent, but now with greater effectiveness, this reduction of rates on quick assets forced monetary institutions into longer-term investments. The way was smoothed for this by encouraging the discount houses to strengthen their capital position by new issues, thus removing the obstacle which had previously stood in the way of a full development of this policy. The process of discount house expansion began already in 1945; in 1946–7 altogether Money Market capital was expanded by 50 per cent. No longer did the discount houses dabble furtively in bonds (to borrow *The Economist*'s phrase); they now made the market for them.

At the same time all financial institutions were adjured not to be shy of holding Treasury bills; in April 1946 Dr. Dalton assured them that a volume of £6500 mn. could not be considered excessive in relation to a total debt of £23,000 mn. (in a sense this was true, but ratios do not tell the whole story). The weekly issue of bills through the tender continued steadily to expand: £140 mn. in January 1946, £150 mn. in August, £160 mn. in September. It would seem however that Dalton was not altogether happy about the size of the Treasury bill issue; opportunities were taken to keep the market allotment manageable by using the departments for tap bills whenever they had funds available, or by causing the National Debt Commissioners to purchase terminable annuities. It would seem also that the famous issue of undated $2\frac{1}{2}$ per cent. Treasury stock in 1947 (immediately dubbed 'Daltons') was designed rather to avoid the necessity for a further expansion of the floating debt than to mop up funds in the market, since its terms were quite out of line with market demands. It was noticeable that after the spring of 1946 Dalton never pressed his belief that the bill issue could safely expand still further.

It was, however, in respect of the mechanism for dealing with the medium and longer-term bond issues that the Dalton technique was especially conspicuous. These issues were required at frequent intervals to refund the now rapidly maturing early war issues; but the terms and occasion of their launching was turned into an important means of forcing down long-term rates. The technique was to 'turn on the tap' at a rate which was definitely lower than that ruling in the market, then to threaten that it would not run for long and that next time the rates would be still lower. If the rate proved initially to be too low the departments would take up the issue and nurse it until the public had become accustomed to the new level. So long as the expansionary process was going on the Issue Department of the Bank and the funds controlled by the National Debt Commissioners (now in full activity as 'The Public Stag') offered an inexhaustible source of funds, since they were repeatedly nourished by fresh doses of inflation.

The greatest success obtained by these forcing tactics was in respect of an issue of 3 per cent. Savings Bonds in the autumn of 1945, right at the beginning of the cheap money campaign; but this issue was at the same time the cause of the most rapid credit expansion, since bank deposits had to be expanded again and again to meet the public's insatiable demand for the bonds. Moreover, the loan did little directly to lower interest rates, since the faster subscriptions were offered the faster flowed the tap. Nevertheless, once the psychology of lower and ever lower rates was established, and the interests of speculators in capital gains (never subject to tax except when figuring for death duties) was thoroughly aroused, in a sense less pressure was needed; a vested interest in keeping them low had been created. This lasted until confidence in the policy began seriously to waver (largely, but not wholly because of international repercussions); even for some little time after confidence had clearly begun to wane cross currents which would temporarily jerk values up again were repeatedly encountered.

Nevertheless repetition of these tactics at lower yields evoked a progressively smaller response, and the Public Stag was increasingly called in to nurse loans. The importance of this—and other—departmental intervention is so great, but at the same time its operation so obscure, that it is impossible to analyse cause and effect in policy with any precision. Thus an issue of funding loan which was mainly taken up by the departments would perform no true funding until it reached the hands of the public; conversely an expansionary movement (or un-funding) could take place if the departments absorbed bonds from the public, even though no change had taken place in the Treasury bill issue. In fact, as can be observed in Chart IV, the long-term interest rate moved down in a series of jerks. The lowest point was touched in January 1947; actually, however, the critical point was the issue of the 'Daltons' in November 1946, since this implied a claim that 2½ per cent. was reasonable for an unredeemable stock (or, more precisely, redeemable only at the government's option); this the public was definitely not prepared to accept.

The immediate effect of the 2½ per cent. Treasury stock was to drive investors into anything offering a slightly better yield and a definite redemption date. The stock of the dying railway companies for instance offered a certain capital gain when it was paid off; even a local authority 2½ per cent. loan was better than 'Daltons', and industrial debentures began to look very much more attractive. Thus in the very short run the manœuvre seemed to have achieved just another turn of the screw in the forcing down process. The tide, however, had definitely turned.

1947 was a year of crises: the fuel crisis of January was to a considerable extent the result of the fickle British climate; but it served to shake confidence in the government's fiscal policy, not only internally, but what was much more important (because it could not be dragooned) externally also. The convertibility crisis of August 1947 was more directly serious because it led to substantial withdrawals of overseas funds, thus worsening the exchanges, although contributing something to dis-inflation. Dalton himself was not entirely proof against the accumulation of adverse factors. In June, following two conspicuous failures of local authority loans offered on the same terms as had succeeded in December, slightly easier terms were conceded for the next comparable conversion; but this too was a dismal failure, all the more noticeable because for the first time since the war it was underwritten in the City and not by the Public Stag. In July the Chancellor's scathing references to 'Baleful Bourbons' did nothing to bring them into line; by August it could not escape notice that references to cheap money were missing from the Chancellor's speeches.

So ended the Dalton experiment. In the end the only gainers were the few speculators who managed to get out in time, and a handful of local authorities and similar trustee borrowers who had their 5½ per cent. and 6 per cent. loans converted to 2½ per cent. at no cost to themselves. The losers were the unhappy savers who invested in Daltons, and in a sense, the great majority of citizens whose interests were damaged by avoidable inflationary pressure and whose freedom was cramped by the very high taxes and the continuance of controls which the policy made inevitable.

In fact from January 1947 the long-term rate had been steadily rising, but just as it had fallen, it rose in a series of jerks which always made it appear that the situation was within an ace of being controllable again. Neither of the two succeeding Chancellors—Sir Stafford Cripps and Mr. Gaitskell—ever resorted to the Dalton forcing methods; nevertheless it was a long while before the official conviction of the always bene-ficent effects of low interest rates was abandoned. But there was a difference in outlook and it was immediately perceived by the City; indeed at an early stage in his Chancellorship Cripps pronounced against the policy of departmental intervention, as it had been used by Dalton, and, as we have seen, he set himself to contain inflation through the instrument of the budget, backed by voluntary dividend and wage stabilization. The official abandonment both of cheap money policy and of the attempt to preserve the national balance without the use of the monetary instrument did not, however, occur until November 1951. By the beginning of 1953 interest rates had reached a level very little different from where they had been left by the storm of the first world war, save that the discount rate on bills, still operating under the control system of the 1930s, remained substantially below the lowest point which it had touched in the 1920s.

It is not possible to carry the story further: but the process of reversing engines followed by Mr. Butler and the Bank of England in the autumn of 1951 is worth noting because it was a continuation of old and new methods, both institutional and psychological. In the first place Bank rate was to be used again after an interval of nineteen years (if we except a few unimportant weeks at the beginning of the second world war); but it would now be used only with discretion and if the situation seemed specifically to require it. Secondly the Special Buyer was not to disappear altogether; he would still be at hand to smooth out kinks as in the 1930s, but he could definitely not be counted on to be always available. Financial institutions would have to learn again to look after their own liquidity. Thirdly (and this was in the short run more effective) a series of funding loans were issued to reduce at a stroke the enormous volume of quick assets, now swollen not only by the aftermath of the cheap money campaign but further expanded to finance stock-carrying in fear of a third world war. This was not necessarily disinflation, but it made disinflation possible. Within the year 1952 the turn of events completed the process.

The Dalton experiment to force ultra cheap money against the trend of markets thus ended in complete failure. It is worth considering briefly, for future guidance, the causes of ultimate discomfiture after such apparent early success. The most obvious cause of failure was the pressure of external events, and the political uneasiness to which they gave rise. It is clear that the major crises: fuel in January 1947 and convertibility in August, arose from decisions which had been taken earlier, and were only partially aggravated by Daltonian policy. Nevertheless it is certain that financial opinion became progressively more apprehensive of the effects of the large credit creation, and increasingly resistant to pressure. Similarly in the later exchange crisis of 1949, when the forcing tactics had been called off but cheap money remained the objective, economic and financial opinion became increasingly restive in face of a policy of financial drift which seemed to have no remedy to offer. A general desire for a return to the use of the credit instrument of policy was clearly building up from the spring of 1951.

Apart from these mainly political considerations there were, however, technical factors which make it unlikely that the Dalton experiment could have succeeded. In the first place it is clear that the 'natural' gap between the short (controlled) rates and the longer rates was substantial and probably widened as time went on, through the increasing need of firms to borrow, as on the one hand their war-accumulated liquid resources became exhausted, and on the other the physical opportunities for new investment improved. On the other side personal cash balances were also being run down, while, as we have seen, penal tax rates and increasing Social Security alike discouraged the creation of new savings. As a result, ever more credit creation was required to attain a given fall in longer-term interest rates. Secondly, the success of the policy depended on the ability of the departments to receive tap Treasuries or to nurse new issues; only while the expansionary process was going on would they be continually nourished with the funds necessary for this purpose. This situation did not really survive the spring of 1947.

Thirdly, and perhaps most important of all, while competition with private stock exchange business could easily be controlled, and the local authorities were completely cut out by legislation of 1946 compelling them to satisfy all their needs through the Local Loans Fund, the requirements of the nationalization programme could not be avoided. The Chancellor was forced to accommodate first, large issues of compensation stock to shareholders, and later, issues for the Public Corporations themselves. In this respect the depressing effect of the two big Transport issues of November 1946 and January 1948 was particularly noticeable. This process continued with increasing intensity after 1948: Gas Stock in May 1949, Electricity in 1950 and Steel in 1951, successively overhung markets. Among all this, however, the most important obstacle to the repetition would seem to be the technical limitations of departmental intervention without a heavy expansion of credit; in most circumstances it is probable that such an expansion would be brought to a halt by the condition of the foreign balance before anything like the volume of the 1946 expansion had occurred.

The Dalton experiment in its later stages was unique as a sustained attempt to force markets in the opposite direction to that in which they were naturally tending and to do so by the use of debt management alone. In some ways it is comparable to the purely monetary attempt between 1925 and 1929 to hold up interest rates against the forces tending to pull them down, but, as we have seen, in this case fiscal policy and debt management were not fully consistent with monetary policy. Both attempts had unfortunate effects on the internal situation and in the longer run had serious international repercussions. In the wholly controlled war economy the methods used were fully justified, and carried with them very little danger; in more normal times the situation is very different. It cannot be doubted that continued credit expansion materially increased the difficulty of obtaining stability by fiscal means, entailing higher taxes and more extensive controls than would otherwise have been necessary.

This is one obvious conclusion which emerges from even such a cursory examination as we have attempted. The interesting factors which emerge, however, are not so much the results of policy, especially of the Dalton experiment, as the new means which have been discovered of obtaining a given end. A mere recital of these inevitably gives an impression that is at once too tidy and too refined. It is not incumbent on the authorities to expound their current debt policy as it is incumbent on the Chancellor to lay his budget plan before Parliament. Much of credit policy goes on behind the scenes and can only be deduced by outward signs (such as changes in the volume of bank deposits). Nor is it in the nature of debt management or credit policy that an entire programme can be drawn up and followed through, as is now attempted in respect of fiscal policy; rather policy proceeds step by step in a process of trial and error.

The old methods of monetary policy were finally abandoned over twenty years ago because change had made them inappropriate: internally through the expansion of the public sector, externally through the failure of the international gold standard on the old basis. Experience since then has shown two things: first, it is more difficult and wasteful to attempt to attain a given fiscal policy without the support of credit control, secondly that a new type of monetary instrument is capable of being built round debt management. Clearly more experimentation in the new methods of control is still needed. It should be the task of the next decade to discover how the new credit instrument can best be co-ordinated with its big brother fiscal policy, now reaching years of discretion. That there should be still unsolved problems need cause no dismay. Of all the lessons which the exceptionally hard school of experience has forced on the life of the generation we have been studying, surely the most important is that of change, and the constant necessity to adapt our institutions to it. Only thus can we assure that the structure of British finances will be such as to get us nearest to the attainment of our aims and ideals.

BIBLIOGRAPHY

GOOD books on the public finances are unfortunately rare. The inquirer's main source of information must therefore remain the statistics published by Government departments and other public bodies. The most important of these are listed below.

Some general histories and biographies contain good accounts of particular episodes in the history of public finance. Worth mentioning are the description in *The Life of Sir William Harcourt*, by A. G. Gardner, of the first introduction of progressive taxation (death duties); and Eli Halévy's *Histoire du Peuple Anglais*, Epilogue II, on the establishment of social security and the progressive income tax in the first decade of the present century. Of fundamental importance in this respect also are the reports of the Royal Commission on the Poor Laws (Final Report 1909). More recently F. A. Shehab, in *Progressive Taxation*, has traced the whole story of the emergence and gradual acceptance of the progressive principle in British income taxes from the second half of the eighteenth century to 1920, when the implementation of the recommendations of the Royal Commission on Income Tax may be said to have established the tax in its present form. On general budgetary history, Sydney Buxton's *Finance and Politics, 1783–1886*, is a unique study year by year of the interplay of politics and finance; but unfortunately it ends too soon to do more than lay the foundation of our present study. Finally, in *The Finance of British Government, 1920–36*, I attempted a general history of the various aspects of public finance and debt management and their interaction for the inter-war period.

On different aspects of social expenditure in the inter-war and more recent periods a number of useful works are available. The P.E.P. Report on *British Social Services* (1937) gives a good account of social insurance as it had developed between 1911 and the outbreak of war. The Report of the Interdepartmental Committee on Social Insurance and Allied Services, 1942: (the Beveridge Report) is fundamental on this subject. In *The Economics of National Insurance*, Mr. A. T. Peacock has drawn attention especially to the problems connected with the rapidly expanding outlay on old-age pensions. In *Housing and the State*, Dr. Marian Bowley traces the course of local authority building throughout the inter-war period. The Ministry of Health and other annual departmental reports give current information on various aspects of the social services; that of the Ministry of Education for 1951 includes a most useful history of public education 1900–50.

On the revenue side the (Colwyn) Report of the Committee on National Debt and Taxation (1927) furnishes a pioneer discussion of a number of modern problems. The Reports of the Royal Commission of 1920 on the Income Tax (mentioned above) and the published papers of the Royal Commission on the Taxation of Profits and Income, now sitting, provide informative discussions of fundamental importance for an understanding of the working of personal income tax and profits taxation. *The Taxation of War Wealth*, by Hicks (J. R. and U. K.) and Rostas, sets out the principles and gives a comparative account of the practice of war finance. Shirras and Rostas in *The Burden of British Taxation* and T. Barna in *The Redistribution of Income through Public Finance* analyse the income distribution of taxes (and in Dr. Barna's case of public expenditure also) on the eve of the second world war.

Exceptionally the field of local finance is relatively well supplied with literature. In *Central and Local Government; Financial and Administrative Relations*, D. N. Chester describes the development of the relevant machinery up to 1951. In this connection, the Reports of the Committee on Local Government Manpower are also important. Three studies written for the National Institute of Economic and Social Research (Cambridge University Press, 1943–45) by J. R. and U. K. Hicks: *Standards of Local Expenditure*, *The Problem of Valuation for Rating*, and *The Incidence of Local Rates in Great Britain*, contain statistical analyses of aspects of comparative local finance. More recently four reports of a joint working party of the Institute of Municipal Treasurers and Accountants and the Institute of Incorporated Accountants have similarly examined the effects of the Equalization Grant of the Local Government Act, 1948.

On the question of budgetary and national balance we are concerned with two different aspects: (1) the principles and practice of compensatory finance, (2) machinery for keeping and presenting the public accounts and for the control of expenditure. On (1) the basic principles were set out with statistical support by Keynes in two publications which appeared in the early months of the second world war: *How to Pay for the War* and 'Income and Fiscal Potential of Great Britain' (*Economic Journal*, December 1939). These represent the epoch-making application of his analysis in *The General Theory of Employment*. More general application of the theory is contained in *Full Employment in a Free Economy*, by Lord (then Sir William) Beveridge and others. In 'The Budget as an Instrument of Policy' (*Three Banks Review*, June 1953) I have set out briefly the genesis of modern ideas of budgetary control. On (2), *The Problem of Budgetary Reform* by J. R. Hicks was a pioneer attempt to rearrange the British Government accounts and methods of accounting, so as to provide an economically meaningful result which would tie in with the National Income estimates and Social Accounts of the Central Statistical Office, and thus form the basis of a policy of national balance. The Report of the Committee on the Form of Government Accounts (1950) sets out the minimum reforms which even a conservative approach admits to be necessary. Two reports of the U.N.: 'Budgetary Structure and the Classification of Accounts', and 'Government Accounting and Budget Execution', describe systems in force in some other countries; the principles set out follow closely *The Problem of Budgetary Reform*. In *The Control of Public Expenditure* (*Financial Committees of the House of Commons*), B. Chubb relates the history of the Public Accounts Committee and of the successive reincarnations of the Estimates Committee.

Hargreaves's *National Debt* (1930) is still the only comprehensive work on the history of the British Government's obligations. The technique of credit control through debt management and other methods is set out in Sayers's *Modern Banking* (third edition 1951). The story as seen by the City can be followed week by week in the pages of *The Economist*. A patient examination by the Public Accounts Committee of civil servants apparently most responsible for debt management (summarized in *The Banker*, January 1953) elicited what almost amounts to a denial of the existence of any technique, and is not the less interesting on that account.

Finally, on statistics, the primary sources for Central Government expenditure are the massive volumes of the Estimates (*ex ante*) and Appropriation Accounts (*ex post*) of the Supply Departments (Civil and Defence) and the Revenue Departments. With the Appropriation Accounts should be taken the reports and comments of the Comptroller and Auditor-General. On the revenue side the annual reports of the Commissioners of Inland Revenue cover death duties in addition to income tax, surtax, and other Inland Revenue taxes. Recently these reports have contained much interesting statistical information, for instance on the distribution of incomes, on profit taxation, and on the composition of estates of different sizes passing at death. The recent raising of the exemption limit for death duties, however, considerably reduces the coverage of this information.

The most important sources for general purposes are those concerned with 'the Budget' in the widest sense: first, the *Financial Statement*, available on Budget night, which sets out the Budget Accounts of the Central Government, a summary of expenditure and of proposed tax changes, with their estimated effect. The *Financial Statement* is supplemented later in the year by the *Finance Accounts*, giving additional details, especially of tax receipts and the Central Government debt position. Secondly (dating from 1941, and containing figures first for 1938) comes the *White Paper on National Income and Expenditure* prepared by the Central Statistical Office and containing integrated accounts, in terms of money flows, of income and outlay in the different sectors of the economy, including the public sector. Since 1952 this account has been supplemented later in the year by a more extensive *Blue Book of National Income and Expenditure*, which gives, in addition, detailed sector capital accounts and some 'break-down' of capital formation by type and sector. Thirdly, since 1947 we have had the *Economic Survey*, giving the broad picture of the nation's economic position and outlook, considered both from the internal and the international point of view; with this should be taken the periodic reviews of the balance of payments position and, dating from November 1953, the monthly publication *Economic Trends*.

Over a course of years the *Annual Abstract of Statistics* (pre-1939, *The Statistical Abstract*) gives summaries of most important aspects of public finance, including the finances of the local authorities and the social insurance funds. Prior to the second world war a *Return of Expenditure on Social Services* (known as the Drage Return, from its instigator) was published annually. A similar but less detailed account has recently been included in the *Monthly Digest of Statistics* for May of each year. This is, however, a poor substitute for the original Return. The Reports of the Comptroller and Auditor-General on the Audited Accounts, together with the Reports and Investigations of the *Public Accounts Committee*, which are based on them, are of first-class importance for criticism of expenditure. Of considerable interest also are the investigations of the present series of *Estimates Committees* (dating from 1947) and of their predecessors, the *Committee on National Expenditure* of the 1914–18 war and the *Committee on Expenditure Arising out of the War* of the second world war. These investigations mainly deal with particular topics.

Tying on to these official statistics, mention should be made also of the current comments of *The Economist* (which is especially useful on monetary affairs) and of the *London and Cambridge Economic Service*, now issued quarterly in *The Times Review of Industry*. Detailed figures of Local Government finance are now published by the Institute of Municipal Treasurers and Accountants.

INDEX